THE 100 YEAR SAVINGS SOLUTION

THE
100 YEAR
SAVINGS SOLUTION

How to Create the Financial Foundation
for Yourself, Your Family,
and Your Legacy

RICK SAPIO, IE
TERESA KUHN, JD, RFC, CSA

LIONCREST
PUBLISHING

THE 100 YEAR SAVINGS SOLUTION
How to Create the Financial Foundation for
Yourself, Your Family, and Your Legacy

FIRST EDITION

ISBN   978-1-5445-3591-3   *Hardcover*
       978-1-5445-3592-0   *Paperback*
       978-1-5445-3593-7   *Ebook*
       978-1-5445-3594-4   *Audiobook*

Contents

Disclaimer

The 100 Year Mindset, The 100 Year Savings Solution, and The Barbell Investment Strategy are trademarks of The 100 Year Company, LLC.

The information provided in this book is for general information only. It is not intended to provide tax, legal, or investment advice, nor to recommend any particular financial instruments, investments, or products. Each person's situation is different. This information should not be used as the basis for making a decision to purchase or sell any investment. Instead, seek advice from your financial advisor regarding your investment decisions and your attorney and accountant regarding legal and tax questions.

Please note the names, situations, and circumstances described in the book have been changed to protect the privacy of the authors' relationships.

Introduction

It was a can't-miss investment opportunity.

At least, that's what Jacob told himself.

He had seen some reasonable investment success in the past, usually when he stayed in his wheelhouse. However, this opportunity was *not* in his wheelhouse—and red flags were everywhere.

The opportunity centered on a company Jacob didn't understand. He didn't know how it operated, and he didn't know how it was supposed to make money. All he knew was that his friend said he couldn't go wrong. He felt horrible that he missed making his millions on Bitcoin, so he was ready for the next "good deal."

Besides, he'd always been told he needed to diversify his investments, so why not?

Jacob took the plunge and invested half of the money he had saved in his IRA account for the past fifteen years—which was $25,000—into the stock of a technology company that he knew very little about. Then, he sat back and waited to collect his returns.

The returns never came.

Not long after that, the stock plunged, and in only six months, his $25,000–investment has plunged down to a value of $1,500—or more than 90 percent down. Not only had Jacob lost more than $20,000 of his hard-earned money, but the mistake set him back years in his savings goals.

As professionals in the financial industry, we've seen countless people struggle just like Jacob over the years. Despite our respective attempts to steer people toward better financial decisions, we still saw them fall into this same Jacob-like pattern time and time again.

But why? What is it about the current system that makes it so hard to get ahead and have your money grow, consistently, over the long-term? Why do so many otherwise careful and deliberative people make rash and ill-considered decisions when it comes to their money?

Why would so many thousands of people—who would normally take months to research the purchase of an automobile in order to save a few hundred dollars—be the same people to jump into the Bitcoin or Token craze and risk their hard-earned money on a whim...or a blog post.

There are plenty of factors at play, but the simple answer is this: investing is complicated and emotional. To be successful at it on your own, you need both the time and the training to do it right.

Unfortunately, time and training are two luxuries that are often in short supply. Between managing their career, running a business or a side hustle, participating in their family activities, spending time with friends, focusing on health, managing all the demands of various screens constantly in their faces, and so on, the average person already has enough on their plate. Most people just don't have the leeway to learn the ins and outs of proper investing. When they do try to learn, they're often left with even more questions than before:

- Where is the best place to invest?
- Should I make the maximum investment into my 401(k) each year?
- Should I trade stocks on a daily basis like others do?
- Should I set it and forget it (i.e., never look at my investments)?
- Should I invest into a small business or a franchise?
- Should I try getting into one of the many real estate investments available to me?
- Bitcoin is hot! Should I learn about cryptocurrencies?
- Should I buy cryptocurrency tokens or NFTs like my friends are doing?
- Should I buy and manage a single-family home or two?
- Should I invest into a home and rent it out by the week on VRBO?
- Should we find a financial professional that we trust to do this for us?

Looking for answers alone is enough to make a person's head spin. With so much conflicting information out there—and so much misinformation as well—how can anyone be sure they've found a strategy that actually works?

When viewed in this light, it's no wonder people like Jacob make what in hindsight appear to be obvious and expensive mistakes.

The good news is that it doesn't have to be this way for you. There's no rule that says saving your money—the right way and for the long-term—has to be complicated. With proper knowledge and support, anyone can learn to become a smart investor and start building a financial foundation to stand the test of time.

All it takes is a new approach to an old problem.

WELCOME TO THE 100 YEAR SAVINGS SOLUTION

In this book, we will introduce you to a new approach to investing that we call The 100 Year Savings Solution. At its core, this philosophy is fairly straightforward: before taking on any high-risk investments (or really any investment for that matter) or before pouring all your net worth into your business, instead start by building a foundation of liquid, cash-based assets. We designed this approach to be low-risk, easy to understand, and good for both your short-term and long-term financial health. More importantly, it simplifies the investing process and keeps you focused on a clear, steady path to prosperity.

To help you understand how The 100 Year Savings Solution

works and how you can adopt it into your own life, we've divided the book into the following two parts.

PART 1: THE 100 YEAR MINDSET

Many investors fall into the same trap as Jacob, losing money on investment after investment and falling further behind on their goals. The mortgage is sometimes paid late, retirement investing gets pushed further out, and your financial future gets murkier and murkier.

This is the trap of short-term, reactionary thinking. When you're only thinking about what you should be doing in the short-term moment, it's easy to lose sight of your long-term financial goals. But in order to escape this trap, first, we have to understand it.

In order to avoid falling into the short-term trap, you adopt a mindset that keeps you focused on your long-term goals. To do that, Part 1 introduces the core philosophy driving The 100 Year Savings Solution: "The 100 Year Mindset."

Here's the basic idea: by focusing on your goals 100 years from now, you can make smarter decisions for yourself in the present moment. By way of an extreme example, let's say that you were committed to living to be 110 years old. You probably wouldn't drink a quart of vodka today. Your commitment to living to a very old age will inform the decisions that you make at this moment.

This long-term mindset also encourages you to think not only about yourself but also about your legacy—what you leave behind for the people, organizations, and causes that you care about.

When applied to The 100 Year Savings Solution, this mindset helps you focus on three key values:

1. **Simplicity:** Investing doesn't have to be complicated. In fact, the best investments are often the simplest ones to execute.
2. **Probability:** Whatever you invest in, there is a high probability that the outcome will be exactly what you expect it to be.
3. **Leverage:** When you apply your time and resources correctly, you will produce the intended result with less stress and time.

With your focus where it belongs, all the other noise, confusion, and chaos of short-term thinking disappear. In its place is a sense of clarity, purpose, and, most importantly, *confidence*.

PART 2: THE BARBELL INVESTMENT STRATEGY

If you don't always make the best investing choices, that's not entirely your own fault. The financial system as it is currently constructed privileges the big players while keeping everyone else off balance. In short, you're encouraged to chase quick wins and leap at whatever interesting new investment opportunity comes your way—whether you fully understand all of the risks that you are taking or not.

In Part 2, we begin by exploring this problematic system. Then, we turn our attention to the second element of The 100 Year Savings Solution, a framework that we call "The Barbell Investment Strategy."

We'll get into more detail in the following chapters, but here's the basic concept. Picture a barbell, just like the kind you would find at a gym: a small light bar in the middle and large plates of heavy weights on each side. These three different parts of the barbell are a metaphor to represent three different areas of savings and investment:

1. **The heavy weights on the left side** of the barbell represent your safe money. Investments here are considered to be very conservative and include cash products, such as CDs, money market accounts, and cash-value whole life insurance.

2. **The light bar in the middle** represents your traditional retirement-related options, such as 401(k) accounts and individual retirement accounts (IRAs, ROTH IRAs, SEPs, etc.). These accounts typically invest into mutual funds, ETFs, the stock market, and the bond market.

3. **The heavy weights on the right side** are your long-term-oriented, higher-risk/higher-potential return, illiquid investments. These include your own business, private companies that you invested into or that you control, real estate, land, private funds (like hedge funds), and other alternative investments.

Whether investors realize it or not, virtually everyone has investments into each of the three buckets described above, *but* it is the proportion that is off for most people. Consider your investments for a moment.

Are they balanced, with the left and the right sides fairly proportionate? Or is it right-side-heavy, with little or no left side at all?

In a perfect scenario, the left side should represent 40 percent of your net worth, the right side should also represent 40 percent of your net worth, and the middle bar of the barbell should represent 20 percent of your net worth.

Most people tend to tie up all their net worth in high-risk investments such as stocks or their own business. This leaves them particularly vulnerable during financial downturns. When banks stop lending—just as they did during the Great Recession that began in 2008 or again during the coronavirus pandemic—these right-side-heavy investors lose their access to immediate, liquid cash.

With a more balanced approach, one that focuses on building a safe-money foundation, built on easy access to your funds, problems like these can be avoided. The Barbell Investment Strategy helps you to set clear savings priorities, no matter where you are on your current financial journey.

CREATING YOUR FUTURE TODAY

In the following chapters, we'll walk you step-by-step through everything you need to know to create your own 100 Year Savings Solution. By making good choices today that will help you save for tomorrow, you will be better equipped to leave a lasting legacy for your loved ones down the road.

Before we get started, however, let's get clear about a few things.

First, this is hard work, designed only for those rare few who truly want to create lasting wealth. You won't find any get-rich-quick schemes here. Investing has a funny way of attracting people who want to make a quick buck, but it usually doesn't work out well for people with a "quick-money" mindset.

This book is for those who are comfortable getting rich slowly—and those who are willing to ask for help along the way. The most successful investors are comfortable having open conversations with trusted partners about what's best for their money.

Second, this book is a challenge to the rigid, traditional ways of thinking about money, long-term wealth, and investing. If you favor traditional approaches above all else, if you believe the only way to invest is through stocks or a 401(k), or if you've already made up your mind about insurance or insurance institutions, then this book is *not* for you.

Finally, this book *is* for those people who are willing to be honest with themselves about their current investment situation. If your current way of doing things isn't working exactly as you want (that is, if it's not putting you on a plan to build generational wealth), if you're tired of making the wrong financial decisions, and if you're tired of all the needless hoops you have to jump through that you don't understand, this book is for you. The first step is being willing to take a good, long look in the mirror and accept that what you're doing may not be working.

If that sounds like you, then it's time for something new without fear of failure.

It's time to stop living for the quick payout and start living for long-term wealth.

It's time to build yourself up so that you can be strong for both yourself and for others.

It's time to create your 100 Year Savings Solution.

PART 1

The 100 Year Mindset

CHAPTER 1

Understanding Our Own Worst Tendencies

"It is not the critic who counts; not the man who points out how the strong man stumbles, or where the doer of deeds could have done them better. The credit belongs to the man who is actually in the arena, whose face is marred by dust and sweat and blood; who strives valiantly; who errs, who comes short again and again, because there is no effort without error and shortcoming; but who does actually strive to do the deeds; who knows great enthusiasms, the great devotions; who spends himself in a worthy cause; who at the best knows in the end the triumph of high achievement, and who at the worst, if he fails, at least fails while daring greatly, so that his place shall never be with those cold and timid souls who neither know victory nor defeat."

—THEODORE ROOSEVELT

Here is a little exercise to get you thinking:

1. Add up all your income over the past twenty years. So, if

you've averaged $100,000 income per year, this would mean that you earned $2 million in total income in the past two decades.

2. Now, do the math and calculate your total net worth—excluding the value of your private business, since it is likely illiquid.

3. Compare the two numbers. How much of the money have you been able to hold onto?

So, using the example above, after taxes, approximately $1.4 million has come directly into your bank account. That's an impressive number!

But now (if you are the average American), look at your total net worth: $125,000. Of the $1.4 million you have taken home, $1.275 million of that money is already gone—and it's never coming back.

Where did it go?

We are using smaller numbers here to demonstrate how this works. You may have an income higher than this, but the same result happens; in most cases, millions of dollars have been wiped out, eliminated, kaput, with zero to show for it!

Almost always, when we have people do this exercise, they are completely shocked at how small their overall net worth is relative to their incomes over the past two decades. They felt like they were on the right path but then quickly realized that they have *not* been good stewards of their income. How did this happen?

For many people, there's no single catastrophic mistake for them to point to. Rather, they made a series of small choices that, over time, dramatically impacted their total net worth. After twenty years of these small, unconscious choices, suddenly they find they're not where they want to be.

If this is you, before reading any further, you have a choice to make: do you want your next twenty years to be the same as the previous twenty?

If so, then put down this book and keep doing what you're doing. There's no need to read any further.

If not, then keep reading. Let this moment be your turning point.

Here in Part 1 of the book, we're going to introduce you to what we call The 100 Year Mindset. As its name implies, The 100 Year Mindset is about long-termism over short-termism. It's about building a stable financial foundation that will last a lifetime (or longer), not about chasing quick returns. Above all, it's about building your wealth with confidence and clarity, so you can enjoy your life and leave a legacy for others.

We'll explore these concepts in greater detail in Chapters 2 and 3. Then, in Part 2, we'll teach you how to translate your 100 Year Mindset into a long-term savings strategy. But in order to move forward, first, we have to understand the mindsets and behaviors holding us back from reaching our financial goals. If you've ever found yourself wondering how you can earn so much and yet save so little, this chapter is for you.

WE ACT UNCONSCIOUSLY

In *The Power of Habit*, author Charles Duhigg argues that more than 95 percent of the average person's actions are unconscious. We don't think about what we're doing. We just react based on a notion either of what we want to do or what we think we're supposed to do. Sadly, this behavior extends to our financial decisions as well. We often don't consider how we spend our money—or more importantly, how we should save it.

Take Bud, Rena, and their three young kids, for example. Eighteen months ago (eighteen months prior to the writing of this chapter), their family brought home a new puppy, which then proceeded to chew through most of their furniture and wreck a number of household items. The experience has been nothing short of a disaster. Without thinking through the problem, the family decided that their dog is probably lonely—so they decided to get another dog to keep company with the first dog.

Another six months go by, and whatever was left of their house is also a chewed-up mess, from their backyard to their furniture to their carpeting. Bud and Rena are miserable. They are not sleeping well at night because of the noises the dogs make— especially after the couple started making their restless pets "sleep" in cages throughout the night.

They are in a lousy situation. They feel that they can't get rid of the dogs now because their children feel the dogs are part of the family. They fight constantly over what to do with their "damn" dogs. They have tried five different trainers, and they've even sent the dogs away to an expensive training camp. Over the past year, they have invested more than $25,000 into their dogs. They are tired, upset, and confused.

Even worse, they feel completely and utterly stuck.

Feeling stuck is a key trait of unconscious behavior. Because we don't think through the decisions that led us to a bad situation in the first place. We often don't understand how we got there. Because of our lack of agency, we feel like we don't have any choice except to suffer through our bad decisions.

Of course, this is rarely the case. Bud and Rena have plenty of options to end their misery. The first option could have been to never bring untrained puppies into their home in the first place, which, of course, they never considered.

So, now what? Well, they could get rid of the dogs. They could commit to training them the right way. They could plan their home and schedules around the reality of pet ownership so that they don't come home to a war zone every day.

Now, what does Bud and Rena's story have to do with money?

A lot.

In our experience, the old adage is true: how you do anything is how you do everything. You're either living your values when making decisions or you're not. This extends to every aspect of our lives—to decisions about pets, to decisions about what to eat for dinner, and to decisions about how we spend and save our money.

When Bud and Rena chose to get first one dog and then another, they acted unconsciously. They didn't think the ideas through. They didn't consider the added responsibility they would be taking on, especially with a young family to also care for. They didn't consider whether they had the routine and lifestyle that would complement their new identities as pet owners. They didn't consider *anything*, and this lack of consideration cost them both money and happiness.

Had Bud and Rena acted consciously on their idea to buy a dog, they would have approached the decision more rationally. In doing so, they might have realized that, yes, they did in fact want a dog, but they weren't ready for pet ownership yet. It would have made more sense to wait another year or so until their kids were a little older and when they could prepare themselves (and the house) for the lifestyle change having a dog would bring.

This isn't to say that acting consciously means you'll get every decision right. Acting consciously means incorporating information into your decision-making process so that you can make informed decisions. It means acknowledging that your emotions often drive your financial decisions, that your upbringing and programming heavily influence how you see the world, and that your ego often drives decisions about money.[1]

WE BUY HIGH AND SELL LOW

Here is one of the oldest bits of financial advice that we've heard our entire lives, but very few people actually act on it: buy low and sell high.

---

1   Libby Kane, "A Financial Planner Highlights One Hard-to-Avoid Mistake That Can Cost You a Fortune," *Business Insider*, June 16, 2015, https://www.businessinsider.com/why-your-emotions-can-cost-you-a-fortune-2015-6.

It's good advice—and if you were to ask most investors, they'd say that's exactly what they do. Unfortunately, whether they realize it or not, the vast majority of us are doing the exact opposite.

To help explain why this strange phenomenon persists, let's look at the story of Stan and Delia, who decided to buy a house a few years ago. As they began scouting locations, they noticed that prices on the south side of town have gone up over 50 percent in the prior year. *What a tremendous investment opportunity!* they thought to themselves. If they can buy a house in that neighborhood now, then they can sell it at a huge profit a few years down the road because, they figured, prices will continue to rise at that pace. They surmised that they can then use the profits on this first house to buy their dream house down the road. Soon, Stan and Delia, using faulty logic, had purchased their first house in this "high-growth neighborhood," and they couldn't be more excited.

But then, something unexpected happened: the housing market changed. Those 50 percent gains regress back to the mean. Stan and Delia kept waiting for the market in their area to rebound, but it never did. When Stan and Delia finally did sell, they sold at a break-even price.

So, what happened? What did Stan and Delia do wrong?

We humans tend to think in straight lines. If we see the value of something go up, we then assume that it will keep going up at the same rate. Stan and Delia bought high because they expected property values to keep climbing higher. Unfortunately, as they found out, that's rarely what happens.

The truth is, when Stan and Delia saw house values go up by 50 percent in the south side of town, they had already missed their opportunity in that area. Prices were already high, with no guarantee that they would be going any higher. If they truly wanted to buy low and sell high, they would have refocused their efforts on finding neighborhoods where property values *hadn't* jumped in the past year, but where the conditions were right for prices to take a big leap soon. But the couple didn't see it that way, and they lost a lot of potential profit as a result.

People make these same kinds of *buy high, sell low* mistakes in the stock market as well—again, even though they think they're doing the exact opposite. For instance, when Apple crossed $3 trillion in market capitalization—which means that the total value of all the stock in Apple put together was worth more than $3 trillion—in 2021, many people rushed to buy Apple stock. But why? The stock value was already sky-high. The stock was sure to regress, and investors had next to no opportunity to double their money. If they really wanted to make a killing with Apple stock, they would have bought low back in the mid-1990s in the days before the iMac, iPod, and iPhone, back when the company was still struggling to get by—and then they would have proudly held the stock for many years, becoming wealthy in the process.

But this is rarely how investors behave. Investors rarely buy low, hold long-term, and sell high. The reason is that, emotionally, it is hard for human beings to operate this way.

This same phenomenon can also be seen in mutual funds. When investors are considering which mutual funds to buy into, they typically look at historical performance. How has the fund done in the past year, the past five years, or the past decade? In reality, it doesn't matter. Past success doesn't guarantee future success—and buying into a mutual fund while its value is high just means you're spending more to see smaller (or perhaps nonexistent) returns. Despite what some mutual fund rating services might say, sometimes the best time to buy a mutual fund is when it is performing poorly, but it is poised to grow in the future.

WE CHASE HOPIUM

Would you rather *hope* that you are building a stable financial foundation, or would you rather *know*?

When Natasha began working with Kristen, her financial advisor, she listed her net worth at $7 million. However, the more Kristen looked at Natasha's numbers, the less they made sense.

Natasha had a $100,000–annual salary at her job. On top of her income, she had also done well investing in real estate, and she had some equity in her home as well. But when Kristen added all these sources up, Natasha's net worth only came out to about $1 million. How did Natasha account for the $6 million?

According to Natasha, that other $6 million came from what she believed her business was worth, but Kristen could see that Natasha's business wasn't worth anywhere close to that.

Yes, Natasha had struck upon an interesting business model, a hair salon business that she had built up to five locations, but her business was only seven years old, it wasn't growing quickly, and it was barely bringing in enough revenue to pay its employees.

Like many entrepreneurs, Natasha was grossly overvaluing her business's actual worth—and in turn, her own financial standing!

It's hard to fault Natasha for her optimism. She believed deeply in her business and in its long-term prospects. The problem is that Natasha was operating without any safety net. Almost her entire net worth—whether perceived or real—was tied up in her business. If the economy tanked—like it did during the coronavirus pandemic—or if her business didn't otherwise pan out as she expected, then she would have to take a massive financial hit.

Natasha may have had a lot of positives going for her, but she was nevertheless in a precarious financial position—all because she got addicted to *hopium*. Someone told her that her business idea was worth millions, she *hoped* that person's estimation was true, and she staked her entire financial future on that hope.

Hopium is a common—but dangerous—reality of investing. Just like falling in love, it short-circuits our rational brains and encourages us to focus only on the positives and the best-case scenarios, warning signs be damned. Of course, when something does go wrong and the hopium wears off, it's easy to see those warning signs and wonder how we could have missed them. But in the moment, we think everything is going perfectly—despite all the indicators that it's not.

Fortunately, Natasha had a trusted advisor in Kristen to catch this error and begin to set Natasha on a safer path. But in the meantime, the damage had already been done. Until Natasha could begin to balance her assets by fully understanding how

The Barbell Investment Strategy works; and until she starts with her safe-money plan on the left side of the barbell, she is exposing herself to a tremendous amount of financial risk.

WHICH PATH WILL YOU TAKE?

Taken in isolation, none of these mindsets and behaviors is likely to single-handedly sabotage your financial future. But then again, no decision happens in isolation.

Just as we saw in the exercise to open the chapter, it's not the one big mistake that hurts most people. It's the little mistakes that, when added up over time, keep us from reaching our savings goals. One day, we make an unconscious choice. Another day, we buy high and sell low. Another day, we get caught chasing hopium. After enough of these days, like it or not, we're not where we thought we would be.

Once you realize this, the question is simple: how do you change?

As we see it, you have two paths.

The first path is to wait and let biology take over. Just as certain hormones shift and dwindle as we age, so too do our more destructive impulses. After all, you're far more likely to see a twenty-five-year-old go all in on a high-risk investment than a sixty-year-old.

Whether he meant to or not, this was the path Alan took. Throughout his life, Alan had made a good living as a doctor, but as an entrepreneur/investor on the side (like many doctors), he had several ups and downs over the years. He made a lot of money, but he also lost a lot of money. But by the time he turned sixty, something had changed in him. Alan no longer had the appetite for financial risk of any kind. He closed his practice, paid off his mortgages, and said, "I'm done. I'm not losing another dime. From now until I die, I'm keeping all my money in the safest investments I can find."

From there, Alan focused all his energy on preserving the money he had. He had a nice home and other properties, and he now owned them outright. But he no longer had any stomach for living a flashy life or for chasing investment returns. He was no longer interested in risk. He was interested in sure things.

This shift isn't uncommon for people entering their retirement years.

Call it biology or call it wisdom gained with age. Whatever the case, their hopium stores are depleted. All they see is what they could lose instead of what they could gain, and they stop wanting to chase risk. Instead, they focus on preserving what they have, which means preserving what they *know* are smart investments, rather than what they *hope* might be.

This is a perfectly acceptable path—that is, if you're not interested in taking an active role in your investing future. The problem with waiting for age and wisdom to kick in is that it forces you to make up a lot of ground in a short amount of time. And depending on the choices you made in the preceding decades, that could be quite a bit of ground indeed.

If you choose this path, we wish you luck. However, if you're still on the younger side and you'd like to stop chasing hopium now, start taking action, and begin building a stable financial foundation, then we'll see you in the next chapter.

GUT CHECK TIME

Some of you may have read this chapter and said, "Surely that can't be me!" Maybe you're right—but you'd better be sure about that. Ask yourself:

1. How much money have I lost from poor investment choices?

2. How much energy, time, angst, noise, and chatter has that cost me in the past?

3. How close am I to achieving my wealth goal amount?

Be honest with yourself. After all, you don't have to prove anything to us—just to yourself. If you're not as happy with your answers as you thought you would be, read on. We can help.

Ready to learn more or talk to our Team? Scan the code above!

CHAPTER 2

Understanding The 100 Year Mindset

"Lack of focus, not lack of time, is the problem. We all have twenty-four-hour days."

—ZIG ZIGLAR

Tony was a rising star in the NBA. In college, he helped his team to become a force to be reckoned with each of the first three years that he played there. In fact, he helped his team get to the NCAA Basketball Tournament's Sweet 16 teams in his junior year in college. As soon as he was eligible for the draft, the NBA came calling, and when Tony signed with a team, he earned himself a tidy $7 million–bonus after taxes...up front.

Wanting to be smart, he found a financial advisor who told him to put the money away where he couldn't get his hands on it. His advisor told him to lock up the $7 million since, in addition to this bonus money, Tony would also be earning $1.5 million per year for the first five years of his contract, as long as he was playing, and not injured.

Tony was interested, but he wanted to be sure he was trusting the right person with his money. For two years, Tony went back and forth with this advisor, doing tremendous due diligence and leaving no questions unexplored regarding this advisor's history.

And then, just when his advisor thought Tony was finally going to follow the path he'd laid out, Tony disappeared, evidently deciding to take his money somewhere else.

One year after the advisor (we'll call him Bob) gave up on Tony, one of Tony's lawyers called Bob to inform him that Tony had a career-ending injury, which also meant zero income in the only career he knew anything about—playing basketball.

That was a devastating blow, but at least he still had the signing bonus money—plus a few million more he had earned and saved before becoming injured. With a healthy seven figures in the bank, Tony still had a chance to grow his wealth and live out the rest of his life comfortably.

But then Tony met Bill, a low-level promoter from Hollywood. After only a few conversations and zero due diligence, Bill was able to convince Tony to invest $9 million of his money into a movie project he claimed to be working on. As soon as Tony gave him the money, Bill disappeared. The movie never materialized, and Tony never saw his money again, no matter how hard he tried to find Bill.

Tony had come so close to making the right decision with Bob, the conservative advisor, but when a person he hadn't vetted presented him with a big, high-risk opportunity, he mistakenly thought he had a slam dunk (pun intended).

Suddenly, that nest egg that Tony thought he could count on the rest of his life was gone—and it was never coming back.

Contrast Tony's story with Sean's. Sean never made more than $60,000 a year. He lived below his means and was very frugal. Furthermore, Sean never looked to make any big splashes with his investments, choosing instead to build a solid, balanced financial foundation. First, he bought catastrophic insurance to protect himself and his family from being sued, and then he bought three specially-designed whole life insurance policies that enabled him to sock away a lot of money with very low-risk but decent, tax-advantaged, and steady returns. Additionally, with the added income that his wife made as a high school teacher, they both maxed out their IRAs and 401(k)s. Whatever money he had leftover, he invested into four small single-family rental properties over the years.

Sean retired in 2019, at the age of fifty-six, with over $4 million in true net worth—nearly double what Tony was worth.

Tony may have had more opportunity than Sean, along with *far more* income over the years, but he took a very different approach to how he managed his money. While Tony went for the big splash and the quick win, Sean opted for monotony, security, and the sure thing.

Dan Sullivan, the founder of Strategic Coach, often says in his speeches, "The faster you can get to monotony, the more successful you will be." Sean understood that when it comes to saving your money, "keeping things simple" should be your rallying cry. Monotony may sound dull and boring, but it's the difference between knowing and hoping. Tony *hoped* for a big return on his high-risk investment, but Sean *knew* he would be able to consistently build his wealth by betting on solid investments.

Sure, beating the same drum day in and day out might not seem that exciting, but do you know what *is* exciting? Success. When building your own financial foundation, would you rather approach your wealth like Tony or like Sean? That is, would you rather bet on the *hope* of success or the *certainty* of it?

In this chapter, we'll introduce you to The 100 Year Mindset. At the core of this mindset is monotony. It's not flashy, and it won't grow your wealth as quickly as other high-potential-return, but often risky strategies. However, by prioritizing long-term goals and values over short-term gains, a 100 Year Mindset offers a surefire, stable path to both personal and financial prosperity.

WHAT IS THE 100 YEAR MINDSET?

In his book, *The Millionaire Next Door*, author Thomas J. Stanley shined a spotlight on millionaires like Sean. This kind of millionaire isn't flashy. They might be worth $3 million or more, but they live modestly. In general, this type of millionaire typically lives in a small house and drives a ten-year-old economy car. They make practical choices, rather than those that would draw attention to themselves.

The type of person described in *The Millionaire Next Door* is the epitome of The 100 Year Mindset. In reality, a 100 Year

Mindset is a philosophy of living that extends beyond financial well-being. In fact, it touches every part of your life, from your relationships to your health, from how you spend your money to how you spend your time.

Like Sean, people with a 100 Year Mindset relentlessly seek monotony, especially when it comes to their long-term wealth creation. They prioritize their mental and physical health by following simple, predictable rhythms over the long haul. In so doing, they avoid chaos, knowing that the more chaos that is present in their lives, the more difficult it is to be present in the moment. And when you're not present, you aren't set up to make the best decisions—whether in your family or with your money.

Someone with a 100 Year Mindset might also exhibit the following traits:

- They stay in their lane by focusing on what they know and what they are good at, and they rarely venture into unknown, risky, or time-wasting endeavors.
- They seek stability in their families and careers.
- They marry right, and they choose friends wisely.
- They focus on their health by eating right, exercising, and keeping their weight in a healthy range.
- They live well below their means.
- They use their time, energy, and money for wealth accumulation.
- They value financial independence over social status by avoiding "keeping up with the Joneses."
- They are self-reliant, and they raise self-reliant, independent, hard-working children.

- They value accountability and responsibility, and they rarely play the victim card.

You may already exhibit some or most of these traits, while others of you may be interested in improving. Embracing The 100 Year Mindset doesn't happen overnight. However, once you set your eyes on a clear long-term vision for your life, you begin to take an active role in your own future. Rather than living unconsciously and taking an ad hoc approach to important decisions, you begin to take an active, conscious role in your own destiny.

To do that, first, you have to get clear on your priorities.

ARE YOU LIVING YOUR VALUES?

Carl was a prominent author and public speaker. A core part of his message was the importance of defining your values and then living them. For Carl, the values that he spoke about often from the stage were God first, family second, health and fitness third, his career fourth, and his hobby, fixing up old cars, fifth.

Carl's message inspired Erik, one of his fans. So, one day Erik flew out to meet Carl for a weekend. Carl arrived at the airport in a limousine to pick Erik up. Then, they were carted off to dinner, where Carl showed off all the bizarre people that he knew. From there, Carl shuffled Erik about from club to club, partying the night away. The next day was more of the same: golf in the morning, meetings in the afternoon, and more partying that night.

At no point did Carl practice his faith. At no point did he introduce Erik to his wife and kids. At no point did he engage in anything that resembled health and fitness.

This got Erik thinking. God first, family second, and health and fitness third were fine values to have. But stating your values isn't enough. You have to *live* them out.

Carl was *not* living his values. But unfortunately, Carl is far from alone in this regard. Be honest: if someone were to follow you around with a video camera for a day, from the moment you woke up in a typical morning, until the moment you went to bed on a typical night, would you be proud of what they recorded—or horrified?

Whether it's the time spent in front of the TV, or mindlessly watching Netflix on the laptop, the time wasted with vices like drugs and alcohol, the hours on "smart" phones and the like, or even on toxic relationships, many of us aren't living the lives we want to be. According to some estimates, many people spend as much as ten to eleven hours in front of a screen each day. Some of this time can be attributed to work, but the rest of that time is essentially wasted.

Each of us only has so much time in the day. Every moment we spend on distractions is a lost opportunity to live out our values and do what's actually important to us. Of course, to live your values, you have to know what they are in the first place.

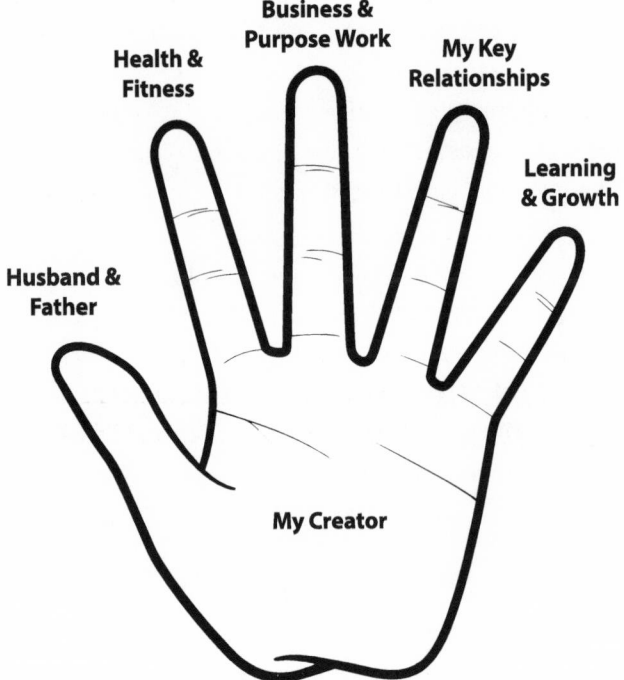

If, like Carl, you're not living up to your priorities, this exercise can help. The concept is simple: Look at your hand. Now, imagine that each finger represents your biggest values or priorities in your life. For Erik, those values are:

- **Thumb:** Being a great husband and father
- **Index finger:** Health and fitness
- **Middle finger:** Career (both purpose/non-profit work and professional work)
- **Ring finger:** Key relationships
- **Pinky finger:** Learning and growth
- **Palm:** His Creator

Your values will no doubt be different from Erik's. Whatever they are, once you've defined them, your goal is the same: spend 95 percent of your waking time dedicated to at least one of these values. If you're ever unsure of what you should be doing, just look at your hand for affirmation. Is what you're doing aligned with your values? Could you be doing something else that's a better use of your time?

If this exercise sounds overly simplistic, that's the point—remember, as unglamorous as it is, The 100 Year Mindset is about chasing monotony. In our conversations with several billionaires over the years, we've found that they all have one thing in common: simple, straightforward lives. This Values Exercise cuts out the senseless noise of our everyday lives and allows you to focus on what matters.

IT'S NEVER TOO LATE TO GET STARTED

If you're reading this and you're fifty, sixty, or older, know that it's never too late to adopt The 100 Year Mindset. The goal of The 100 Year Mindset isn't to get you thinking about what you're going to be doing 100 years from now, but to encourage you to take a long-term view of your financial life and your personal life and to consider what kind of a legacy you want to leave behind for the people you care about.

In the next chapter, we'll teach you how to apply The 100 Year Mindset to your financial legacy by focusing on the three core values of The 100 Year Savings Solution: Simplicity, Probability, and Leverage.

GUT CHECK TIME

If you're unsure if you're making the best use of your time, you don't need a camera crew to follow you around to find out. Just try one of the following approaches:

1. At the end of your day, write down everything you did that day. Repeat this process for as long as a week.

2. As you review all the things you did in a particular day, decide what you can do to either eliminate it, delegate it to someone else, or automate it (as in finding a way to have it be done without your involvement). Only continue to do those things that are fully and completely aligned with your values.

3. Every fifteen minutes or so, throughout your day, stop to consider what you're working on and what you're thinking about. Is it what you're meant to be working on, or are you distracted?

A narrower version of this exercise can be applied to your financial goals as well. Ask yourself:

1. Did my money decisions for the day align with my long-term goals?

2. What about over the past week? The past month? The past year? What should I be doing differently?

You owe it to yourself to spend the necessary time to write out your answers to these important questions. The more you do these simple exercises, the more focused you will be on achieving your long-term wealth goals. In Part 2 of this book, you will learn about The Barbell Investment Strategy, which will give you an easy framework for success.

Ready to learn more or talk to our Team? Scan the code above!

CHAPTER 3

Prioritizing Simplicity, Probability, and Leverage

"Treat your money like you would treat a canteen of water in a trek across the desert."

—ROSS PEROT

Jay and Daria are husband and wife working in two different cities. Their offices are seventy miles apart from each other. One works on the west side of Fort Worth, Texas, and the other has an office on the east side of Dallas. Because of this extreme distance, they decided to buy a home that is roughly equidistant for each of them to drive, which, if their home was between their offices, they would each have to drive thirty-five miles. But unfortunately, without thinking clearly about it, they decided to buy a home on the north side of the Dallas/Fort Worth (DFW) International Airport.

On top of that, their dream home needed work—a lot of work.

THE 100 YEAR SAVINGS SOLUTION

So, for the next several months, they committed to a full renovation of their home and property.

The house is approximately sixty miles away from each of their offices, and even further away than where they currently live.

At each decision point, Jay and Daria thought they were making the right choice. However, they never fully considered the complications they were introducing into their lives:

- Both of them will regularly have to spend between one hour and two hours every day commuting to and from work.
- Home renovations are expensive and time-consuming, and they rarely go as planned, not to mention planning meetings with contractors at the house at odd times during the day.
- Daria is pregnant with their first child.

They're aware of each of these considerations, of course, but they're committed to this path, in part because they don't feel like they have any other options. They do. For instance, they could make a conscious effort to work closer to each other or to arrange to telecommute part-time, i.e. working from home. If flexible work arrangements aren't an option, they could purchase an already-built home that more effectively splits the difference between their two offices. Instead, they opted to *rebuild* a home that is far away from both of their jobs, making for an approximately sixty-mile commute for each of them.

They put on brave faces and decide to push ahead with their plan anyway. The next year of their life was a complete disaster, a fresh hell of one new challenge after the next. Between wrangling contractors, deciding on features, commuting, and

48   www.100YearSavings.com

preparing for their little bundle of joy, all of Jay and Daria's time is spent, and their mental capacity is shot. Moving into their dream home, it turns out, has been a total nightmare.

Meanwhile, down the block, June and Jeremiah have just moved into a brand-new house that was turn-key ready—and that even came with a warranty on the work. Their home-buying process was easy too: all they cared about was getting a property that was close to a good school for their kids (and that had separate closets for the couple). They found a house that fit the bill, they liked the way it looked, and they bought it. They also opted to take lower salaries to get jobs that would allow them to work forty-hour weeks from home. For them, there are no hour-long commutes, no wrangling with contractors, and no consternation about how to set up their nursery. Just happy evenings on the front porch, listening to music and watching the sunset.

What's the difference between these two couples? What is the key difference that made one home-buying experience so miserable and the other so painless?

June and Jeremiah are "long-termers." Instead of basing their decisions on their whims or what sounded nice, they followed three guiding values: Simplicity, Probability, and Leverage.

Simplicity, Probability, and Leverage are the foundation of The 100 Year Mindset—and therefore The 100 Year Savings Solution. When you're a "long-termer," all decisions radiate out from these three values, whether that decision has to do with your family and relationships, your business, or your money. Without them, it doesn't matter what else you try; your results will be inconsistent at best. To understand why, let's take a closer look at each of these values and how they impact our financial decisions.

CORE VALUES OF THE 100 YEAR MINDSET
SIMPLICITY

Simplicity means predictable patterns. Simplicity is knowing your routine and sticking to it. Simplicity is the epitome of chasing the mundane. When Simplicity is the dominant value in your life, decisions are easy.

Rick's adherence to simplicity has characterized his career at every turn. For instance, when he was offered his first job in New York City, Rick walked out of the building, looked around, spotted a "For Rent" sign, and moved in. For the next few years, all he had to do was wake up, get ready for his day, and take a brief walk to work. Simple.

Rick also brings this same spirit of simplicity to his relationships. For instance, for the past two decades, he and his wife have gone out to dinner every Monday night at 7:30 p.m. for their weekly date night. They go on their date after they sit down as an entire family while their kids eat dinner at 6:00 p.m. at home. Rick and his wife have chosen Monday for their weekly date night because the town is quiet, the restaurants are mostly empty, the service is great, and everything is simple. All Rick and his wife have to focus on during their date nights—in addition to the occasional fight about their differing parenting styles—is reinforcing their connection to each other. The babysitter knows; the neighbors know; the kids know; everyone important knows: *Monday night at 7:30 p.m. is date night for Melissa and Rick!*

Even when organizing events, Rick makes Simplicity his guiding prinçiple. Every year, whenever possible for annual events, he directs his planning staff to keep all the details the same—the same hotel banquet room, the same floor plan, the same schedule, the same food. While his staff sometimes worries that this sameness might bore attendees, the result is the opposite: every event is more successful than the last because the guests know what to expect from the brand offering. The guests come away entertained, well-fed, and happy.

Think about it. Why do you often use similar companies and products for years and years? The reason is that you know what to expect, and you've come to appreciate what to expect.

Here's the secret power of Simplicity. When the core factors of an event, a decision, a company, or a relationship all remain fixed, there are no surprises and no guesswork. Everyone knows the game plan, freeing them up to focus on executing to the best of their abilities. Sure, certain details in the overall approach may change as necessitated but never without sacrificing the core value of Simplicity.

The same is true when planning out your wealth-building strategy for your life. By settling on well-understood financial instruments that have stood the test of time for more than 100 years, by working with a proven system like The Barbell Investment Strategy, and by creating a "set-it and forget-it" plan of execution, you get the simplest of all worlds, which allows you to live your life with much less stress—and with much more confidence!

PROBABILITY

Probability is about being clear on your objectives and creating the highest likelihood decision-making that will achieve that objective (i.e., increasing the *probability* of achievement).

Here's how probability works. Imagine, you're a sophomore in high school and it's your fifteenth birthday. On this day, your grandparents tell you that you are going to receive your $50 million–inheritance in thirty-five years, on your fiftieth birthday.

How do you think that knowledge might impact your decisions for the next thirty-five years of your life? Would it change your ambition? Your priorities? Your appetite for risk? Would it be more probable that you save up your own money in those intervening years or less probable?

This is a challenge many face when leaving a legacy behind for their loved ones. They want to provide for their family, but they don't want to create any dependencies in the process. The question is: how do they approach this situation so that they can impact future generations the way they hope to?

It all comes down to your everyday decisions. If you are the grandparent preparing to leave behind a substantial windfall to your grandkids, what can you do to decrease the Probability they will squander it or become less motivated because of it?

One way would be to begin working with your grandkids to teach them how to save their money. That way, they can learn how to manage money, respect money, and learn to grow their money long before they receive any inheritance.

Increasing your Probability of success isn't the work of a day, but rather of a lifetime. This kind of focus can be a challenge, but it's a cornerstone of The 100 Year Mindset—and essential to meeting your long-term goals.

For instance, in Chapter 1, we began with an exercise encouraging you to examine your net worth. Through that exercise, we learned that it usually isn't one mistake that can sabotage your long-term financial goals but rather a series of small choices that add up to a big impact.

If your goal is to save $1 million by the time you're fifty years old, then every time you make one of these small, harmful spending choices, the probability of you achieving that goal diminishes. As a value, probability speaks directly to these everyday choices. Will you choose to increase the probability that you will meet your goal, or will you torpedo that goal and buy a brand-new luxury car instead?

LEVERAGE

Leverage is using your existing relationships, infrastructure, technology, and rhythms that are already present in your life in the service of achieving your goals.

To explain how this value works, let's use the story of our doctor friend, Asa. Asa has done well in his career, and recently he's become more interested in putting his existing savings to better use.

Thinking it will be a good investment, Asa decides to buy the building that houses his private practice. All his friends and peers told him it was the right thing to do, and several other doctors he knew had followed the same path.

What Asa didn't realize is that, by buying his building, he just took on a considerable amount of additional responsibility in an industry—commercial real estate—that he knows nothing about. Walking into this deal, Asa didn't know the first thing about owning commercial real estate and all the challenges that come with it. Suddenly, he's spending every spare waking moment trying to manage his small real estate business (because owning a commercial building is akin to owning a separate business). In addition, he still has to manage his young family and his medical business. He begins to find it difficult to come up with the extra money each month to pay the commercial mortgage and insurance bills.

How did things go so wrong so quickly? Simply put, Asa didn't stay in his wheelhouse. He had no existing knowledge, expertise, or relationships he could leverage to become a successful commercial real estate owner. Asa was right to see what else his savings could do for him, but he sank his money into something he didn't understand.

If Asa wanted to leverage his existing relationships, infrastructure, technology, and rhythms in order to grow his wealth, he had other options that would have been right in his wheelhouse. For instance, he could have invested in his partner's medical device company. This would have created leverage in several key ways: Asa has known his partner for twenty years, he understood how the devices work, and he knew the company had a high Probability of success.

Alternatively, if Asa *was* dead set on owning his building, his first step would have been to identify his Leverage points. Who else did he know who had purchased their buildings successfully? Could he partner with a real estate investor? Should he hire someone to manage the property for him? By identifying these Leverage points and taking the responsibility off his own shoulders, Asa would have given himself a much higher Probability of success.

Of course, if Asa were following our Barbell Investment Strategy (see Chapter 5), he would have first built a stable financial foundation for himself with cash reserves and a specially-designed, 100 Year whole life insurance policy.

That way, whether his investments succeeded or failed, he would still be on solid ground. Minimizing risk, after all, is one of the key results of using the Simplicity, Probability, and Leverage values set.

LET'S START BUILDING YOUR BARBELL

Now that you understand The 100 Year Mindset, you are halfway there on your journey to creating your very own 100 Year Savings Solution. In Part 2, we will start by exploring the dangers of the traditional investing model. Then, we will introduce you to a new model based on Simplicity, Probability, and Leverage, which we call The Barbell Investment Strategy.

Our Barbell Investment Strategy takes the core concepts of The 100 Year Mindset that we've discussed in Part 1 and applies them directly to your long-term savings plan. If you're unhappy with the status quo, and if you are not concerned with the approval of traditional financial planners...*and*, if you're okay with going against the traditional Wall Street investing model, then consider The Barbell Investment Strategy the alternative savings solution you've been looking for.

To be clear, The Barbell Investment Strategy, or Barbell Strategy for short, is not some wild or fringe concept. In fact, it's quite the opposite. As more people feel burned or ignored by the traditional savings and investing system, the Barbell Strategy offers an alternative that is focused on building a solid financial foundation based on stable assets. To help others plot their paths forward to a more stable future, we must first take a look back to the past, to a time before high-risk investments and market-driven retirement vehicles dominated the financial landscape.

If you're ready to learn more, we'll see you in Part 2.

GUT CHECK TIME

Do you have Simplicity, Probability, and Leverage in your life? Here's a way to find out. Ask yourself:

1. Do I make my decisions consciously or unconsciously?

2. How often do I feel overwhelmed?

3. What negative people or things that give me stress will I commit to removing from my life?

4. Would others describe my life as chaotic? Why? How can I simplify the chaos?

As you review these questions, what will you do in order to fully embrace Simplicity, Probability, and Leverage in your life? Hopefully this chapter gave you some ideas about how to attain it. The next step is to commit to it; embrace the benefits and philosophy that come with it.

Only then will you be able to execute your own Barbell Investment Strategy and build a more stable financial future for yourself and your loved ones.

Ready to learn more or talk to our Team? Scan the code above!

PART 2

The Barbell Investment Strategy

CHAPTER 4

The Business of Separating You from Your Money

"People rarely make the same mistake twice; they usually make it twenty or thirty times."

—ANONYMOUS

If you were to look at a typical photo of Americans at the beach during the 1970s, you might be surprised at what you see. Virtually everyone you see in the photo is thin—and many of the people are in excellent shape!

Contrast that with similar photos of Americans in the present-day decade post-2020. If something looks different to you, you aren't imagining it.

Between the 1970s and the 2020s, something changed in the way the average American ate and took care of themselves. As

"Frankenstein" foods went mainstream and fast-food chains endlessly expanded, so did our waistlines. We went from a largely fit, active society to an overweight, sedentary one.

Our health and well-being aren't the only things that have taken a turn for the worse since the 1970s. As a population, our ability to save money has suffered as well. Up through the 1970s, thanks to a strong pension and insurance system, a majority of Americans were disciplined, successful savers who regularly set aside between 8 and 10 percent of their income and watched it grow over time.

However, sometime during the 1980s, things began to change, and approximately three out of every four Americans now have little to no savings. They live paycheck to paycheck, with no concrete plan for how they will sustain themselves during their retirement years.

So, what happened? How did we go from a society of savers to a society of spenders?

Welcome to the world of business—or more specifically, the business of separating you from your money. Wherever you go in the investment world, it seems that whomever you encounter—whether salespeople, banks, or Wall Street—people are doing what they can to make sure they have more of *your* money and that you have less.

This isn't inherently bad practice. It's the whole nature of buying and selling, upon which our entire economy is built. However, there's a good way to practice capitalism and a not-so-good way. If someone separates us from our money, and provides value in return, then we don't mind. This scenario is called a fair exchange.

However, if someone separates us from our money and we get nothing out of the transaction, then we mind a lot since we got ripped off.

No one wants to get ripped off. And yet, when it comes to saving, investing, and managing money, that's exactly what happens to far too many people. We are encouraged to put our money into high-risk investment accounts; while at the same time, we are discouraged from building a stable financial foundation first.

Does this approach ever benefit the people who try it? Sure. If you have built wealth and are working from a stable financial foundation, there is absolutely a time and place for some risky investments. But for reasons we'll explore both in this chapter and throughout the book, it's important that you manage risk responsibly—and with your eyes wide open.

The truth is that banks and brokerage firms aren't in the business of helping you succeed; they are in the business of separating you from your money—or, better stated, of earning significant fees by "managing" your money. And as we'll see in this chapter, if you don't have the time, knowledge, or capacity to manage your money correctly, that's exactly what's going to happen.

In this chapter, we're going to look at the dominant philosophy of savings and investing that most contemporary brokers and financial advisors recommend. Our goal isn't to persuade you away from participating in this system entirely. In fact, as you will see in the next chapter, we have made room for elements of this approach within our Barbell Strategy. The problem, however, is that the contemporary model encourages quite a bit of unnecessary risk. By first building a stable savings foundation, you can invest from a position of strength, rather than from a position of need. But as you'll see, that's not what many of us are encouraged to do.

THE RISE OF THE 401(K)

Depending on your age, the way you save for retirement likely doesn't employ the same strategies that your parents or grandparents used. Back in "the old days," a person would get a job that usually came with a defined benefit plan, which is a pension plan that pays you a set amount each month in your retirement.

In some pension plans, for instance, once you had worked for a company for a certain amount of time—perhaps twenty years—you would receive a pension each month, which amounted to a certain percentage of your monthly salary for the rest of your life.

The pension plan was a win-win for both company and employee. Companies won by securing years of longevity and hard work from their employees, reducing the considerable costs associated with firing, recruiting, and hiring new talent. Employees won by knowing that they were literally set for life once they had contributed to their plan for a certain number of years.

Unfortunately, the pension system was vulnerable to attack—and employers often suffered the consequences. Through legislation and enforcement by governing bodies like the SEC and IRS, pensions became too risky a proposition for many businesses, so they began looking for an alternative.

Enter the 401(k). In 1978, a man named Ted Benna discovered the 401(k) inside of an old piece of legal code that had existed for decades. But its potential as a retirement vehicle had gone unrealized until businesses began looking for an alternative to the pension system. Unlike with pensions, the 401(k) transfers the investment risk from businesses to their employees, requiring them to make direct contributions into their own retirement plan—their 401(k)—rather than rely solely on their pension plans and Social Security to carry them through their golden years. Employees were told that, by investing a certain amount of money every year, they could grow their money faster than a pension could, and then they could retire in greater comfort. Even better, they could manage their retirement plan themselves!

This all sounded great in theory. There was just one problem: human nature.

THE PROBLEM WITH ALWAYS CHASING RETURNS

In Chapter 1, we explored some of the common mindsets and behaviors that lead to bad decisions about money. In short, we humans aren't always the most rational stewards of our own money. For many would-be investors, a combination of emotional decision-making and a lack of training makes us generally horrible money managers—even when our money is parked in what should be a stable savings vehicle.

Take the IRA and the 401(k), for instance. The common wisdom

THE 100 YEAR SAVINGS SOLUTION

is that these vehicles tend to generate returns in the range of 6 to 8 percent—or more—annually. This is true to a degree, but there's a problem: a significant percentage of Americans cash out their retirement accounts early.

Here's the problem: when you cash out your retirement fund early, not only do you pay all the taxes that were due on it, but you also pay an additional 10 percent in fees. This is bad news for you but terrific news for the government, who makes countless millions in fees each year. It's no wonder, then, that they've created such favorable conditions for people to buy into these retirement products! Americans would do much better with their IRAs and 401(k)s if they left them alone. But many don't—rendering their potential for bringing strong returns all but moot.

Unfortunately, we aren't much better on the open market either. According to DALBAR.com, the average annual return for the average investor is right around 2 percent.[2] Already that's not an especially encouraging number, but it only tells half of the story. Once you factor in inflation, taxes, and trading costs, the actual take-home for the investor is down to a fraction of a percentage point annually. You got that right: less than 1 percent per year. Ouch!

There's another problem with DALBAR's average: it accounts for *all* investors. This means that outsized successes of famous investors like Warren Buffet are pulling that average way up. Suffice it to say, only about 10 percent of all investors are skilled at what they do and are able to generate wealth consistently in

---

2   "Quantitative Analysis of Investor Behavior: Summary of Returns," DALBAR, accessed January 2020, http://www.qaib.com/.

66   www.100YearSavings.com

the stock market. If you pull that 10 percent of highly successful investors out of the data set, the average return for the remaining 90 percent would be far lower than 1 percent annually, net returns. In fact, as we've discovered through our conversations with many CPAs over the years, a majority of investors actually see negative returns, almost every year.

For the top 10 percent of investors—the people for whom investing is their full-time job—the Wall Street system can be incredibly profitable. However, it's also incredibly risky. Unless you're able to put a significant amount of time—as in full time—into learning the inner game of Wall Street and you understand how to maximize returns within it, relying on the financial brokerage industry to help you generate long-term wealth is a losing bet.

BROKERS WIN, INVESTORS LOSE

In the Wall Street system, the average investor often loses money—whether it's because they cashed out too early, because they made risky investments in a system they didn't understand, or because they didn't buy low and sell high (and instead bought high and sold low; see Chapter 1). This begs the question: if the average investor stands to lose in the current system, who stands to gain?

The large brokerage firms do.

For years, brokerage firms have thrived on the myth that they were putting investing back into the hands of the people. To draw in everyday investors, they offered zero-commission investing services. Unfortunately, this no-commission offer was nothing more than a Trojan Horse. These firms know that the average investor has poor returns over time—in turn, they know that they can profit from their customers' losses, indecision, and over-trading every step of the way.

Commissions or no commissions, brokerage firms make money off their clients' money in a surprising number of ways. They profit by charging interest or transaction fees on almost everything. They even make money on fees when clients sell at a loss.

However they do it, the end result is the same: more money for them and less money for the investors they claim to be helping.

As the data shows, this is big business. In 2017, for instance, the stock market was up 23 percent overall, but the average investor return was only 3 percent that year.[3] That massive difference can be explained in part by two major factors. The first factor is that investors have a pesky habit—as we've explained—of buying high and selling low (a phenomenon we'll explore in greater detail in the next chapter). Even in years where the market sees large gains, individual investors can still end up losing. The second factor is what we've been discussing: all those maintenance, management, and transaction fees—not to mention paying taxes as well—add up fast. To these brokers, then, it doesn't matter if it's an up year or a down year; they're going to profit either way!

Knowing this, it's no wonder that these firms invest billions of dollars in advertising and marketing, crafting sentimental commercials that tug at your heartstrings so that you think

---

3   Ibid.

they have your best interests in mind. They don't. At the end of the day, these firms are just like a casino: they want to separate you from your money, and they have a whole array of tricks designed to do precisely that. And, as we'll see in the next chapter, it works because they know many of their customers are emotional decision-makers who will act against their own self-interest.

It's no wonder, then, that, as exemplified by the rise of the 401(k) over four decades ago, these brokers have gone all-in on the idea of putting investing back in the hands of the people. Unfortunately, it's the people who have paid the price. Once the long-term savings conversation shifted from the company-controlled pension plan to the individual-controlled 401(k) and IRA, Americans began taking bigger risks with their money, leaving their long-term financial stability on shaky ground.

The pension system worked because of its simplicity. The 401(k) system might have sounded good to investors, but it inadvertently added a tremendous degree of complexity (and chaos) into the retirement savings process. Seeing what his brainchild had done to the average American, Benna eventually disowned the 401(k) altogether.[4]

FORGET THE CONVENTIONAL WISDOM

Let's return our attention back to that picture you imagined of people on the beach in the 1970s. What happened to America's waistline? How did things change so drastically in a matter of only

---

4   Sarah Max, "The Inventor of the 401(k) Thinks It Has Gone Awry," Barron's, November 16, 2018, https://www.barrons.com/articles/ the-inventor-of-the-401-k-thinks-it-has-gone-awry-1542413142.

THE 100 YEAR SAVINGS SOLUTION

fifty years? Simply put, as the food system became industrialized
and commercialized, the messaging around food completely
changed. Americans were encouraged to eat processed foods—
"fake" foods. We were told that sugary soft drinks would make
us happy, that sugary cereal would entertain us, and that a bucket
of fried chicken would bring our families back together.

That shift has been wreaking havoc on our health, on our bodies,
and on our happiness ever since. But here's the truth: the people
who choose to buck the so-called conventional wisdom of the
modern food system are happier, healthier, and live longer lives.

The same issue can be found in the way most Americans are
told to invest. In the current system, you're told to take a two-
pronged approach.

First, you're encouraged to load up on our IRAs and 401(k)s.
When you do so, not only do you often benefit from employer
matching, but you also enjoy some useful tax breaks. That much
is true. However, many of us are not given the proper training
to be successful within this system—and many of us cash out
early, nullifying any benefits this approach might have pro-
duced, along with paying penalties and taxes.

Second, you're encouraged to make investment decisions on
your own, whether with online accounts, with a Wall Street
broker, through private companies, or through real estate. Any
of these options *can* bring high returns on your investment, but
they can also be complete busts. The current system encourages us to ignore those risks and consider only the potential
returns. That way, it's just like the food system—concerned not
in the people it serves, but in the profits it can extract.

70   www.100YearSavings.com

Most likely, this isn't new information. Many Americans don't trust the food system, just like many Americans don't trust the financial system. And yet, they participate in both anyway. Why? Because they don't think they have a choice.

If you've made it this far into the book, one of two things is true: you've either already been burned by this system, or you have come to suspect that it may not have your best interests in mind.

But here's the good news: you *do* have a choice, and there is still time to change.

In the next chapter, we're going to teach you the secret of The Barbell Investment Strategy—the key to The 100 Year Savings Solution. This simple process will help you to create a stable financial foundation that will sustain you through the rest of your life and allow you to leave a financial legacy for generations to come.

CHAPTER 5

Introducing The Barbell Investment Strategy

"A government big enough to supply everything you need is big enough to take everything you have."

—THOMAS JEFFERSON

Imagine you're a business owner and that your company's estimated value is $5 million. That's great news for you, but here's the problem: that $5 million is illiquid, which means that it's worth $5 million to *you* and only to you. Can you turn that business into $5 million in cash tomorrow? Of course not.

It takes time, effort, and energy to sell a private business. All that time, effort, and energy devoted to selling a private business can take you, the business owner, away from the one thing that matters most: actually running your business!

When viewed in this light, selling a business can actually become one of the most destructive things a business owner can do in their quest to find cash. They get so focused on selling that they alienate the most important people in their life—namely their family, their clients, and their employees. Naturally, this is a big dilemma.

Without—in this case—the $5 million in cash from the sale of the business to balance out your assets, you're not in a very stable position. The second your business has a couple of bad years in a row because you weren't focused, you risk finding yourself in a free fall with no safety net to catch you.

Unfortunately, many business owners end up in this exact situation. Why? Because, as we discussed in the last chapter, they've been conditioned by mainstream financial thinking to believe that they should always focus on generating high returns on their money, and so they lay it *all* on the line in their business. They erroneously believe that all they have to do is be willing to take a little risk, invest in a business, build it up, and then sell it.

That kind of thinking is wrong.

No one should have 80 percent, 90 percent, or more of their net worth tied up in the valuation of their illiquid small business.

Instead, it's about the *return* of your money. And to guarantee that return, you need to build a balanced, stable foundation. Only then—once your low-risk, solid financial foundation is built—can you move forward and, at some point down the road, chase risk with confidence.

To help you do exactly that, we've created The Barbell Investment Strategy. This investment strategy is built around the core values of The 100 Year Savings Solution: Simplicity, Probability, and Leverage. It is simple to execute. It is highly probable that it will do what we say it's going to do. And it leverages your time and resources in a way that produces the intended result without over-stretching you. You're no longer beholden to what you don't know, you're less likely to fall victim to the latest scam, and you're more confident in the decisions you do make.

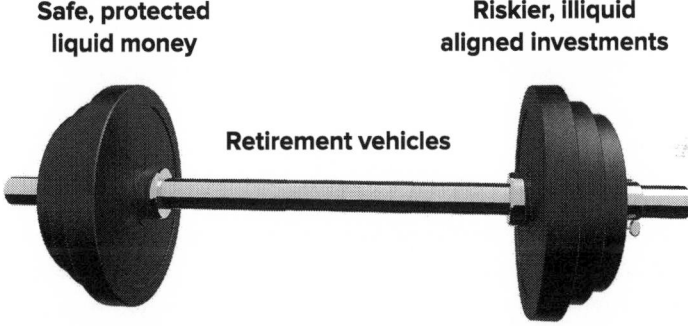

Safe, protected liquid money

Riskier, illiquid aligned investments

Retirement vehicles

The Barbell Strategy can be broken down into three elements:

- **The left side of the Barbell:** This is your safe-money foundation of liquid assets. By focusing here first and building up a large pool of liquid "safe money," you will be better positioned to pursue other riskier investments later on in your life. The goal is to put only solid, conservative, guaranteed investments here. These are proven strategies that have as many benefits as possible. This left side is the step that the vast majority of us forget. We usually jump into investments in the middle and right sides and become unbalanced from an investment perspective for the rest of our lives.
- **The middle bar of the Barbell:** The skinny bar in the middle represents all the various and normal retirement vehicles, like 401(k)s, SEPs, and IRAs, which are typically invested

into the stock market. While these investment vehicles don't work well long-term as stand-alone strategies to bring enormous wealth later in life, they bring benefit in our strategy by bridging the left side of the Barbell with the right side.

- **The right side of the Barbell:** These are your higher-risk, illiquid assets that have the potential for much higher investment returns over the long-term. These investments can include the value of your own business, stocks that are very familiar to you or your skillset, investments into other private companies in which you have a high degree of confidence, commercial real estate or rental properties, etc. The right side has the potential to make you a lot of money long-term.

The Barbell Investment Strategy works whether you're twenty-five and just starting to grow your wealth or you're fifty-five and interested in taking a sounder approach with your money as you approach your retirement years. No matter what you've been doing up to this point, if you decide to pursue this strategy in earnest, the approach is the same: start by building up your left side so that all future financial decisions proceed from a stable foundation.

We'll explore the ins and out of how to set up your Barbell in the next chapter. For now, let's take a closer look at each section of the Barbell, so you can see how the pieces all fit together.

MORE ON THE LEFT SIDE

By the time their kids had left for college, Arnold and Katarina had saved up $525,000 in CDs at their local bank, and they decided they were ready to start actively growing their wealth.

But instead of taking a moment to consciously think through their strategy (remember Chapter 1?), they started throwing their money around carelessly. First, they invested $175,000 into Katarina's brother's start-up medical device company they knew little about. They respected Katarina's brother, who was a successful surgeon, but he spent most of his working hours in surgery, not in building a start-up company.

Next, they invested another $250,000 (approximately $125,000 each) into two separate single-family rental properties. They were told that both were can't-miss opportunities since they were found and managed by another family member who had a real estate management company. In both cases, they put their faith into family members.

Arnold and Katarina thought they were making smart decisions with their money, but in reality, they had set themselves up for disaster. They didn't have a real plan. They didn't do serious research on these opportunities sourced by family members, and neither one of them were experts in either real estate or medical devices. As a result, before they even knew what had happened, they were way out of their wheelhouse and exposed to far too much risk.

Unsurprisingly, none of these initial investments worked out. Only a year later, after they were able to get some of their money out of these investments, they had reduced their hard-earned and saved $525,000 down to a value of $200,000—which was now all that was left of their savings.

Far too many people do things like this for two main reasons. First, they often listen to the wrong people. Second, they think it is far easier to build wealth with get-rich-quick ideas than it really is.

Like many people in their situation, Arnold and Katarina had the right idea. They had accumulated some wealth, and they wanted to see that wealth grow. However, they didn't approach the process with any clear strategy. They knew nothing about the Barbell Strategy and the focus on *safe money first*. They heard that they should start to take some risk with their money, and that they should diversify when they do, but that was as far as their thought process went.

What Arnold and Katarina didn't realize was that they had already built out the left side of their Barbell. That $525,000 in liquid assets would have given them a solid financial foundation—all they had to do was keep that money in stable, liquid savings vehicles that earned a predictable, fixed interest rate, no matter what the markets were doing.

For instance, they could have invested all of their $525,000 in a specially designed whole life insurance policy from a highly rated, mutually owned insurance company that is more than 100 years old, and that has never missed a dividend payment, despite wars, depressions, and pandemics over the years. Such a policy would have paid tax-deferred interest and would be guaranteed to pay at least 4 percent per year, or more, for the rest of their lives. Such an approach would not only have been simpler, but it also would have carried considerably less risk. Also, they could easily borrow against this policy if they need cash for something else. That way, they wouldn't run up against the kind of "liquidity crisis" that often happens in illiquid investments. Unfortunately, they hadn't known that this path was available to them.

We'll explore the value of investing in a whole life insurance policy in Chapter 7. For now, here's the point. Once you have a solid financial foundation on your left side, it's permanent. As long as you manage it correctly, you never have to rob Peter to pay Paul. You have built a platform that you can use to move forward with confidence.

This is the inherent value of the Barbell Investment Strategy—and where it departs most sharply from traditional approaches. Conventional wisdom would tell you to chase growth and to chase risk as quickly and aggressively as you can. However, as we've seen with thousands of investors over many decades who use this safe-money, foundational approach, the left side of the Barbell is the very best way to ensure you have a high probability of creating wealth for yourself and your family over the next 100 years. Focusing on your safe-money foundation first will free you up to then invest and grow the rest of your long-term, private capital on the right side later.

MORE ON THE MIDDLE

The center of the Barbell holds your investments in your traditional long-term savings vehicles, such as your IRAs, 401(k)s, and other liquid, publicly-traded assets, like stocks, bonds, and mutual funds. This could include real estate as well, but only in terms of publicly traded investment trusts (normally called REITs) allowed within the context of your IRAs or 401(k)s.

As we explored in the last chapter, 401(k)s and IRAs are some of the most common investment vehicles around. As such, you likely already have a head start building out this area of your Barbell Strategy. If this is you, we'll discuss how to balance out the rest of your Barbell in the next chapter. For now, it's okay to keep putting money into those accounts—and maximize them out if you can. This is especially true of your 401(k) account, in which companies often will add money into your account in the form of a matching deposit, up to a certain amount each year, so be sure to take advantage of that if your company does this.

But wait, didn't we warn you against investing in these vehicles just a chapter ago? Yes and no. Investing in a 401(k) or an IRA *can* be a smart choice. You just have to remember a few things:

1. **Your consciousness:** be conscious of what you're investing into by staying as conservative as you can, and don't chase returns (e.g., buying something after it has already gone up considerably).
2. **Your hold period:** have a long-term hold period in mind when you decide to buy something to avoid trading in and out.
3. **Your need for cash:** don't cash out early, which will cause you to pay penalties and added taxes.

Finally, regarding the middle bar of the Barbell, don't rely on these investment vehicles as your sole means of growing your wealth. By taking a smart, balanced approach to these investment vehicles in the middle, and by committing to them long-term, you can avoid the common traps that many people fall into and make them well worth the investment to become a stable part of your Barbell.

In other words, don't forget the three core values of The 100 Year Savings Solution: Simplicity, Probability, and Leverage. As long as you don't touch your IRA or 401(k) accounts until you've reached retirement age, you'll avoid incurring any penalties for cashing out early. When it comes to these accounts, then, our advice is to look, but don't touch. Resist that temptation to cash out early in order to buy a house, invest into a business, or dump money into some other illiquid asset.

MORE ON THE RIGHT SIDE

On the right side of the Barbell are all your illiquid investments, such as your business, other businesses that you want to help grow, and real estate. Anything else related to your business that leverages your expertise or your business's expertise—and that is also illiquid—also goes on the right side. These illiquid investments have a higher expected return over a very long period of time than any investments on the left or middle of the Barbell.

On their own, they'd be tremendous gambles that likely wouldn't be worth the risk, especially if you haven't built up the left side or the middle of your Barbell. However, when you're investing from a position of strength—that is, when you've built a solid, stable foundation on the left side of your Barbell that is chugging away at 3 or 4 percent interest a year—the risk becomes much more palatable. Rather than an unconscious gamble, it's a calculated risk.

Here's how an investment on the right side looks in practice. Say you've just started a business. After investing $250,000 as seed capital, your goal is to manage that business effectively so that at some point in the future, you can sell it for a high return. For instance, after ten years, you might sell your business for $5 million—earning you back your invested capital and then some. It's a classic wealth-growing strategy but also a risky one. First, your business has no guarantee of succeeding or selling. Second, while your money is in the business, it's illiquid; you couldn't extract it without considerable effort. This is precisely why it's so important to build out the left and middle side of your Barbell first—so you can leverage money that you're not depending on for anything else.

Also on the right side are real estate investments in rental or commercial property. This can be a great investment, but it can also be a nightmare. Many inexperienced investors aren't ready for all the time they will spend managing their property, nor are they ready for the risk exposure. This is precisely why more experienced real estate investors often participate in a fund, such as a REIT, in which a real estate expert manages the details.

This isn't to say that investing in business and real estate is inherently bad. Ultimately, success in real estate comes down to Simplicity, Probability, and Leverage. If your financial foundation is built, the investment is solid, and you are able to Leverage existing relationships to invest safely, then it can absolutely be worth your time.

By way of example, we'd like to show you how the right side can play out in a more predictable way using the strategy and values that we've outlined so far.

If you are going to invest in or start a private company, the best first step is to ensure—to the highest degree possible—that you start a company that has a high Probability of being sold for a lot of money later. One way to do that is to know *in advance* who the likely buyers of your business might be.

Most people who start businesses have absolutely no idea who would buy their business, when, and for how much. This is poor planning.

Rick has a friend, William, who used to work at Google. This friend knew that Google was interested in buying companies that created recurring revenue business models in the digital advertising industry. So, with a large exit price in mind from his former employer, he created his marketing company.

Exactly six years after he started the company, he was approached by a broker who shopped his company around, and he was able to sell it—not to Google but to a private equity fund, for $32 million. It took eighteen months to go through the entire sales process, but $32 million is a ton of money for owning a company for only six years.

This is a clear example of using Simplicity, Probability, and Leverage as operating values, which will maximize your chances of building significant wealth.

The best part of this example is that William and his wife already had more than $350,000 saved up in a specially designed, dividend-paying whole life insurance policy. They also had over $50,000 in the bank *before* they started their business. This is what gave them the confidence to pursue this entrepreneurial dream. These two clearly understood the Barbell Strategy, and they executed it to perfection.

ALWAYS KEEP YOUR EYE ON THE HORIZON

You now know the basics of the Barbell Strategy. In the next chapter, we're going to show you how to build a balanced Barbell, whether you're starting from scratch or you've already been saving and investing for decades. But before we do, we want to share a story that exemplifies the value of The 100 Year Mindset.

When Benjamin Franklin died in 1790, he gifted his two favorite cities, Philadelphia and Boston, $5,000 each—with the stipulation that they could invest the money, but they could not cash out any of the money for 200 years.

Each city took a slightly different path to investment. Boston chose to minimize risk and maximize proceeds. Philadelphia, meanwhile, loaned the money to others, in small chunks.

By 1990, when the two cities finally got to collect, Boston's original $5,000 was worth a whopping $4.5 million, and Philadelphia's original $5,000 was worth $2 million![5]

So, a $10,000-initial investment grew to $6.5 million cumulatively. Interestingly enough, these accounts were earning only low, single-digit interest rates per year. However, when you let money sit for the long haul, and you don't touch it, even a small amount can turn into a huge part of your wealth accumulation later.

So, it wasn't that the interest rates were especially high on these accounts. It was the fact that compounding interest was able to do the hard work of growing the money. This story demon-

5   Stephan A. Schwartz, "Ben Franklin's Gift That Keeps on Giving," HistoryNet, March 22, 2018, https://www.historynet.com/ben-franklins-gift-keeps-giving.htm.

strates the power of building a stable, conservative foundation before pursuing risk with the rest of your money.

Of course, you won't have the benefit of growing your money for 200 years like Boston and Philadelphia did. Still, even if you're only saving for twenty years, it's amazing how quickly a $5,000-investment can grow. So, let's set you on the path toward growth.

GUT CHECK TIME

Now that you understand how The Barbell Investment Strategy works, it's time to start considering how it might look in your own life.

1. If you did nothing else but focus on the left side of your Barbell, how long would it take you to build up a sizable amount of safe money?

2. What investments can you sell out of now in order to start building up your left side?

3. What can you rearrange in your finances and investments in order to begin building your own Barbell Investment Strategy, the right way?

The beauty of the Barbell Strategy is that it's easy to get started. All you have to do is focus your energy on building up your safe, cash money reserves first—which is easy to do no matter how old you are or whatever the current state of your finances looks like. In the next chapter, we'll show you how it's done.

Ready to learn more or talk to our Team? Scan the code above!

CHAPTER 6

Building Out Your Barbell Strategy to Create Wealth

"Only when the rules are clearly defined can true creativity and success flourish."

—ATTRIBUTED TO VOLTAIRE

If you've already been saving and investing your money for several years—by pouring all your money into your business or by maxing out your IRAs and 401(k)s—then you already have the beginnings of a Barbell. But chances are, it's either incredibly "middle-heavy," or "right-side-heavy."

We're going to let you in on a little secret: Rick was no different. When he was young, Rick took a right-side-heavy approach with his money. His college roommate, Barry (who began selling whole life insurance in his early twenties), tried to talk some sense into Rick. At the time, Barry was advocating for an approach to begin growing his wealth early. In retrospect, his approach was very similar to the left-, safe-money-side of the Barbell Strategy.

"Build up your net worth first by purchasing a whole life insurance policy while you are young," Barry said. "Once you have your asset pool, you will have it forever." To prove his point, Barry then shared the story of his uncle, who had saved up over $3 million by investing his money into a whole life insurance policy.

Rick was young, aggressive, and unimpressed. He told Barry that he believed it was better to start a company and then invest into safe-money investments later in life, after making big money in his liquidity event when his company was sold.

That future date never came. There was never one big liquidity event. Instead of landing on that one big hit, Rick saw a series of small hits—all beneficial but not enough for him to build his foundation the way his friend Barry had recommended. However, when he was forty-five, in 2007, Barry was finally able to get Rick to start a policy, and that policy has grown nicely over the years.

In 2012, when Rick met Teresa Kuhn, who was one of the top producers in the nation for this conservative, specially designed, dividend-paying insurance, Rick realized that he needed to further beef up the left side of his Barbell. Since they met, Rick has added ten more policies, and he now has a total of eleven policies that protect his business and his family, in the most conservative way he knows, while still paying decent interest along the way.

Rick's story is not uncommon. We often live our lives hoping, even expecting, that some big event will come along to make us wealthier than we could have imagined. For most of us, that one single moment will never come.

But here's the good news: it doesn't need to.

That "big event" is a myth. The 100 Year Savings Solution isn't about betting your current net worth on one big payout that will build your wealth down the road. It's about taking a proven, reliable long-term approach to growing your net worth. Build your foundation first, then fill in the rest later, as we've explained.

In this chapter, we'll explore some basic best practices to help you get started creating your Barbell, or to start creating balance in the Barbell you already have. Whatever camp you fall into, remember this: no matter how old you are and no matter where you are in your financial journey, you can always pivot your financial strategy to bring more balance to your Barbell. After all, as long as you're still breathing, it's never too late to change.

This doesn't mean blowing up whatever you've been doing and starting over. Instead, it's just a matter of refocusing your strategy to build out your foundation before you proceed any further in other areas. Long-term, the goal is to create balance with your Barbell—a stable bar in the middle and roughly equal wealth on the left and right sides. Short-term, the goal is to build out your left side as quickly as you can so that you're on safe financial ground.

PRELIMINARY WORK

Before you set out to build your savings foundation, you have to make sure your basic needs are met. If you can't afford to buy a new roof or a new air conditioning system without putting those expenses on credit, then you need to do some basic work to get your expenses in order first.

First, buy a catastrophic insurance policy to protect you if something bad happens. These policies are less expensive than you think. Find a good insurance agent and ask them about this.

Second, build up six months' worth of cash for emergency expenses and put this money in a safe place risk-free. We recommend keeping two months of "ATM cash"—that's right, real, green cash—in a safe place. Then, put the other four months' worth of cash into a savings account at the bank. Make a promise to yourself that you won't touch this money unless it is absolutely necessary. (And if you do touch it, make yourself a promise to pay it back as quickly as possible.)

Having an emergency fund like this will help build your confidence. You know that no matter what, you've got green cash stashed away and ready to be accessed in a moment's notice. This will build your confidence more than you can imagine. Try it!

One note if you're a business owner. Don't just set aside six months of living expenses for yourself, but also six months of operating expenses for your business. Bill Gates was a big proponent of this philosophy in the early days of Microsoft. Even though they were just a fledgling company, he always made sure they had at least a year of expenses set aside to be used if the company went through a period of zero revenue. This was the safety net that allowed him to build his business with confidence. Even if times got tough, he could be sure that it would be a while before his company would be forced out of business.

IF YOU'RE STARTING FROM SCRATCH

Think of saving like you're rolling a snowball down a mountain. The younger you are, the higher you are up the mountain—which means the larger your snowball will be by the time it reaches the bottom. The older you are, the farther down the mountain you are. You can still end up with a large snowball at the end, but you'll need a larger one to get started. You have more money but less time to get going.

In a perfect scenario, you would begin your savings journey by building out the left side of your Barbell first. The left side is all about liquidity. It is your foundation built on safe money that is easily accessible. It is also tax-advantaged. Tax-advantaged means that your money will build up and compound year over year, without paying any taxes. In the end, when you're much older, you'll start to pay taxes as you use the money. This is a much better way to grow wealth—paying taxes at the end, as opposed to having taxes removed at the end of each and every year.

Once you've built up your left side, which can happen quicker than you think, you'll begin to feel wealthy and successful.

When you're starting from scratch, the first move is simple: put your money into stable investments on the left side of the Barbell, such as the ones we've described.

THE 100 YEAR SAVINGS SOLUTION

From there, move to the middle. Max out your IRAs and your 401(k)s—especially if you have employer matching, which is when your company will match the amount that you put into your 401(k) each month. Employee matching is like free money. Check it out for yourself. It's amazing how many employees don't take advantage of 401(k) employee matching.

These traditional savings vehicles—if managed correctly—can be positioned to be low-risk and safer in the long term than the riskier investments you would be making on the right side.

Once your left side is built up and secure and you've maximized your IRAs, 401(k)s, and those types of investments available to you, then the remainder of your money can go toward higher-risk investments on the right side of the Barbell. If you can focus on investing into private companies in areas that you know and understand (remember, it's all about Leveraging your time and expertise), you will set yourself up for the highest Probability of creating long-term, 100 year wealth.

IF YOU'RE MIDDLE-HEAVY

If you're in your forties, fifties, or older, then you likely already started saving years ago. Good for you! Now, the next step is to get your Barbell balanced.

Again, there's no sense in blowing up what you've already been doing. If you've been building out your IRAs or your 401(k) for years, don't cash them out prematurely or otherwise move money out of them. Keep doing what you're doing.

But consider your next steps carefully. Instead of thinking about

92   www.100YearSavings.com

risky investments (which we've warned you about throughout this book), first, focus *all* of your energy on building up a huge balance of safe-money wealth on the left side.

Imagine for a moment that, five years from now, you have more than $500,000 sitting in a policy at one of the largest and highest-rated insurance companies in America. This money is fully available to you since you can easily borrow against it as long as it's set up correctly using The 100 Year Savings Solution formula.

Wouldn't this money allow you to have more confidence in your future? That is what this program is all about. Our goal is to help you replace the financial fear of the unknown with confidence about a higher Probability wealth formula for the long term.

For most people, we suggest a goal of $500,000 on the left side. If that gets you excited, you are the type of person that is perfect for The 100 Year Savings Solution because you're in it for the long haul.

IF YOU'RE RIGHT-HEAVY

This is the most common Barbell scenario that we see. Suffice it to say, if you have $2 million or more in illiquid or risky investments, and you have only $25,000 total available in cash, then you are *way* out of balance.

This scenario is far too common in America.

Right-side-heavy investors are those who put very little focus on their safe-money, or left-side, investments. The vast majority of their investment energy is focused on the right side.

In our experience, there are two main types of right-side-heavy investors. The first type is people who treat their home as an investment and pour all their money into it, thinking that this could be their wealth-building engine. Let's be clear: investing in real estate *is* one way to build out the right side of your Barbell. However, investing in real estate does *not* include the home you live in. Your home is your home. It's a liability, not an investment, so don't view that as a right-side investment.

We've seen moderately wealthy people sink almost their entire net worth into multimillion-dollar homes, both in order to keep up with the Joneses, and because they are under the mistaken belief that they would be able to sell these homes for a big profit later in life. These people don't realize how truly expensive it is to own and maintain a very large home over the long haul.

Don't forget, real estate is considered a high-risk investment for a reason: there's a good chance you won't see any returns on your money. Add in the psychic and reputational energy that so many people invest in their homes, and you've got a recipe for disaster.

The second type are those who view illiquid assets like their golden goose. For many business owners, the dream is to work hard, build a lot of value, and then sell their business for a healthy return. However, if you're taking a large amount out of your business every year for your salary to support your lifestyle—say $500,000—plus the business is paying for your car and other expenses, then you must be careful. You may find that if and when you sell your business in the future, even a large check like $5 million may not provide you with enough return to support your lifestyle.

In this example, if you do receive $5 million, once you're done with taxes and other fees, you'll likely have only $3 million or so remaining. Even if you were able to find a stable investment return of 6 percent per year (which means you are taking on some risk), that will only give you about $110,000 after taxes. There are a ton of ifs in this example, plus some risk, and you end up with far less income each year.

If this will be the case, then selling your business may not be the best option. Ask yourself, *Would it make more sense to keep my business, hire an operator to manage it at a high level, and still maintain my lifestyle?*

This is a mindset shift for many business owners. Instead of looking at your business and thinking about what it *could* be worth if you sold it, think of it as an income stream. If you keep that business (and keep it well-managed), then you are able to keep the income stream.

Here's why this matters: as long as you're invested, all your assets on the right side are illiquid. However, if your business or real estate property is generating income, then you can use that income to focus on moving those monies to the left side of your Barbell and balance out your assets. By shifting your thinking around your business's role in your savings plan, you will be able to reduce your risk exposure and grow your wealth faster.

IT'S TIME TO START SAVING

Throughout this book, we've spent a good amount of time talking about how we humans often invest emotionally or unconsciously. We often don't put a lot of thought into much of what we do on a daily basis, we just act on impulse. By being conscious of the behaviors, we can reduce their power over us, but we can never eliminate them entirely.

That's why the Barbell Strategy is so important. By focusing on the left side and the middle first, you will have a stable foundation of safe money so that you are free to pursue higher-risk investments on the right side later.

It is *very* important that you understand the difference between these two words that are so often considered to mean the same thing: savings and investments.

To us, *savings* are monies that you store in places that have little or no risk with predictable, fixed annual returns and with as many other benefits as you can get. For example, The 100 Year Savings Solution, which uses a conservative, specially designed insurance product, would be considered a form of savings.

On the other hand, *investments* are monies that are placed at risk, with no guarantee of ever seeing this money again. People often underestimate the risk they are taking with their hard-earned money when they are making investments.

It is very important that you understand and internalize this difference between savings and investments. That way, you can become a more disciplined and savvier practitioner of The 100 Year Savings Solution.

Now that you understand how this strategy works and how to apply it to your own situation, you're almost ready to get started creating your own 100 Year Savings Solution. In the next chapter, we're going to take an in-depth look at the core element of The 100 Year Savings Solution: whole life insurance.

GUT CHECK TIME

By now, you likely have a good idea of where you are with your savings strategy and where you want to be. Now it's time to start taking action! Ask yourself:

1. What is the difference between *savings* and *investments*?

2. How much money do I have in savings right now?

3. How much money do I have in investments right now?

4. At this stage in my life, and considering what I'm learning, how much money *should* I have—ideally—in my savings right now?

The Barbell Investment Strategy is simple to utilize and helps you avoid the chaos and moving parts of traditional long-term savings and investment plans. If your Barbell isn't where it should be—if you have too much money in high-risk investments and not enough money in savings—that's okay! The 100 Year Savings Solution can be adapted to wherever you are in your life and wherever you are with your savings. As long as you approach the next steps consciously, you'll be able to make up that ground in no time. No financial solution is one-size-fits-all, so please discuss positioning your assets this way with a member of our Team. They will walk you through setting up your own, one step at a time.

Ready to learn more or talk to our Team? Scan the code above!

CHAPTER 7

Understanding Whole Life Insurance

"Invest in yourself. Your career is the engine of your wealth."

—PAUL CLITHEROE

For many people, the term "insurance" comes with negative connotations. That wasn't always the case. Like receiving a pension fund at retirement (which was very common for many employees), life insurance—and dividend-paying whole life insurance in particular—used to be a cornerstone of the average American's wealth-building and savings strategy (see Chapter 4).

Unfortunately, also like the pension fund, perceptions around life insurance began to change sometime around the 1980s. Where life insurance used to represent security and peace of mind, today it's practically a bad word—even though it's good for us!

Why is that? What has happened over the past several decades?

There are many things that have changed to enable this. In our minds, whole life insurance represents long, slow growth over time, like Benjamin Franklin's gifts to Boston and Philadelphia.

Our entire culture has shifted from slow to fast. We need everything *now*, from gourmet food delivered to our door, to information and media at our fingertips 24/7. This cultural shift has not been a good thing. It is well-known that anxiety and depression are at all-time highs—across virtually all age groups—in our country right now.[6]

Regarding pensions, this warped, fast-first mindset compels us to ask, *Why invest each year into a pension plan that will pay us at some far-off time in the future when we can take that same money and buy tech stocks now?*

This new cultural reality is the antithesis of our thinking around The 100 Year Savings Solution.

Plain and simple, we believe that life insurance has a perception problem. First of all, it's "far too conservative" in many brokers' and financial professionals' minds. Many times, even financial professionals have the same cultural biases toward *now* that the rest of society has. They don't fully understand the *why* behind The Barbell Investment Strategy and The 100 Year Savings Solution.

---

6   Tom Porter, "Anxiety, Stress, and Depression at All-Time High Among Americans: Study," *Newsweek*, April 18, 2017, https://www.newsweek.com/recession-mental-health-depression-anxiety-585695.

Additionally, life insurance as a broad concept tends to get lumped in with all the other kinds of insurance available to people—such as medical insurance, car insurance, and home-owners' insurance. Each may be valuable on its own, but each expense adds up. When people begin to see how much money they are paying for their different insurance products, they often become frustrated with the whole effort.

Second, many people feel that insurance is a rip-off. If you've ever had a claim that went unpaid, then no doubt you know what we mean. It doesn't matter if it was an auto insurance claim, a home-related claim, or something else. To the undiscerning eye, all insurance gets lumped together—so if one insurer ripped you off, you're likely to think that all insurance companies and the policies they sell are nothing more than a giant scam.

We sympathize. It's not much fun to pay high monthly premiums for health insurance that fails to cover all of your medical expenses. It's not fair to pay for insurance on your car, only to be hit with a high deductible the moment you actually need it. It's also not fair to saddle whole life insurance with these preconceived notions. Just because your health policy may have burned you, that doesn't mean your whole life policy will. Yes, the two products may both be a type of insurance, but in virtually every important way, they are very different products with very different objectives.

In this chapter, we'll explain why a dividend-paying, whole life insurance policy from a highly rated company (some of ours are over 100 years old) is a crucial building block for the left side of your Barbell—and therefore, your 100 Year Savings Solution.

THE 100 YEAR SAVINGS SOLUTION

NOT ALL INSURANCE IS THE SAME

When most people think of life insurance, they often think of universal life insurance, rather than whole life. The reason for this is simple: that's what the life insurance industry wants to sell, and that's what they incentivize brokers to push.

Universal and whole insurance are fundamentally different products. Perhaps the key difference is that universal life insurance mixes risk with insurance, while whole life does not. Whole life insurance takes zero stock market risk and has a fixed return that is guaranteed by the insurance company.

Further, universal life policies do not give certain basic guarantees, which means that the policy owner assumes all the risk. Because the investment returns of universal life policies may be tied to an interest rate, a stock market index or a mutual fund, many of these policies fail to produce the intended results, and many clients walk away with serious losses. While universal policies advertise a higher return or annual interest rate, those returns are solely dependent on whether or not the underlying products perform as expected. If they don't perform well, which often happens, then the policy owner is out of luck. The risk of the policy performing is on the policy owner, not the insurance company.

With variable universal life insurance, you're investing in various mutual funds that are held inside of an insurance product, which is both risky and unnecessary. The insurance company is charging the fee for the investments held inside the policy, which can often be expensive. On top of that, they're charging for the death benefit (the actual insurance payment that your estate will receive upon your death). Furthermore, you have

102   www.100YearSavings.com

very limited choices as to how you can invest since you have little control over which investments are actually available to you inside your policy. Here again, it's important to remember the distinction between savings and investments (see Chapter 6). Since these insurance policies are on the left side of your Barbell, you definitely do not want to take risk by making investments here. Unfortunately, that is exactly what universal life insurance policies do—they take risks with your money!

This defeats the whole purpose of building a safe-money foundation on the left side of your Barbell, and for that reason alone, we would not recommend it. Again, this comes back to the values that we promote in our program—Simplicity, Probability, and Leverage. Mixing risk with insurance is not Simple, Probable, or Leverageable. If you want to invest, go invest. Put your money into an account where you get a broader range of investment options than you ever would in a life insurance policy. It will be cheaper, and you will pay fewer fees.

As we'll see in the next section, a dividend-paying, whole life insurance policy is the simplest, safe-money option because the insurance company takes zero stock market risk. Furthermore, the balance sheet of the highly rated insurance company will guarantee a fixed return to you, as they have for more than 100 years, through world wars, famines, pandemics, and natural disasters.

DESIGNING A WHOLE LIFE INSURANCE POLICY TO ACHIEVE A SPECIFIC OBJECTIVE

Not all whole life insurance policies are the same. Depending on its design, the focus can be one kind of benefit over another.

Let's take a dive into what that looks like for both a forty-five-year-old male and a forty-five-year-old female. We'll start with a forty-five-year-old male.

FORTY-FIVE-YEAR-OLD MALE, GOOD HEALTH, NO TOBACCO

Policy Year	Age	Net Annual Premium	POLICY A: Whole Life Insurance + Death Benefit		POLICY B: Whole Life Insurance + Death Benefit + Paid-Up Additions Rider		POLICY C (Recommended): Whole Life Insurance + Death Benefit + Paid-Up Additions Rider + Term Insurance Rider	
			Annual Cash Value Increase*	Total Cash Value*	Annual Cash Value Increase*	Total Cash Value*	Annual Cash Value Increase*	Total Cash Value*
1	46	$25,000.00	$0.00	$0.00	$11,692.00	$11,692.00	$17,218.00	$17,218.00
2	47	$25,000.00	$0.00	$0.00	$12,833.00	$24,525.00	$18,887.00	$36,104.00
3	48	$25,000.00	$17,840.00	$17,840.00	$22,375.00	$46,900.00	$24,314.00	$60,419.00
4	49	$25,000.00	$22,554.00	$40,394.00	$25,434.00	$72,334.00	$26,533.00	$86,951.00
5	50	$25,000.00	$29,866.00	$70,260.00	$29,831.00	$102,165.00	$29,463.00	$116,415.00
10	55	$25,000.00	$36,066.00	$230,588.00	$37,365.00	$269,678.00	$37,441.00	$285,140.00
15	60	$25,000.00	$45,691.00	$437,676.00	$47,811.00	$486,283.00	$47,925.00	$502,583.00
20	65	$25,000.00	$55,020.00	$687,835.00	$59,547.00	$756,642.00	$60,324.00	$776,724.00
25	70	$0.00	$43,227.00	$885,551.00	$47,541.00	$973,924.00	$48,798.00	$999,680.00
30	75	$0.00	$53,906.00	$1,133,175.00	$59,286.00	$1,246,259.00	$60,854.00	$1,279,217.00

*Annual Cash Value Increase and Total Cash Value assume that dividends are paid every year and based on dividend interest rates as of December 2021. Dividends are not guaranteed and can change. The three policy examples on the charts compare three whole-life policies on a healthy forty-five-year-old individual. Results may vary.

This is an actual life insurance illustration based on 2022 dividend scales from a mutually-owned insurance carrier used by the authors.

Policy A:

Your premium goes directly to the death benefit. This design allows for the maximum amount to your beneficiary upon your death but minimizes the policy benefits you can leverage while you are still living.

Policy B:

In Policy B, a Paid-Up Additions Rider is added, allowing your premium to be split between the death benefit and the cash value. This design provides a smaller death benefit short term but increases the benefits that you can Leverage while you are still living, such as accessing the cash value.

Policy A and Policy B can certainly provide you with long-term benefits. However, the whole life policy we recommend is designed to give you maximum cash value in Policy C.

Policy C (The 100 Year Design):

In addition to adding a Paid-Up Additions Rider, Policy C also adds a Term Insurance Rider. Along with the whole life death benefit, the Term Insurance Rider allows you to get as much death benefit as Policy B, at a lower cost. This frees up more dollars to go to the Paid-Up Additions Rider, maximizing the cash value growth.

This special design of a 100 Year policy offers you the highest Probability of generating the most cash value, while being a safe-money savings vehicle on the left side of your Barbell.

Look closer at Policy C above and compare it to the other two scenarios. When starting with a $25,000–contribution in the first year, you'll notice that for your first three years, the overall value increase is relatively modest. However, beginning in the fourth year, everything changes—the growth only accelerates from there. By the tenth year, the policy is already quite valuable. By the twentieth year, the exponential growth is clear. This is the value of a whole life policy designed to maximize cash value: easy access to cash throughout the life of the policy and exponential and clear growth without market risk.

Now let's take a look at how the three scenarios compare for a forty-five-year-old female.

FORTY-FIVE-YEAR-OLD FEMALE, GOOD HEALTH, NO TOBACCO

Policy Year	Age	Net Annual Premium	POLICY A: Whole Life Insurance + Death Benefit		POLICY B: Whole Life Insurance + Death Benefit + Paid-Up Additions Rider		POLICY C (Recommended): Whole Life Insurance + Death Benefit + Paid-Up Additions Rider + Term Insurance Rider	
			Annual Cash Value Increase*	Total Cash Value*	Annual Cash Value Increase*	Total Cash Value*	Annual Cash Value Increase*	Total Cash Value*
1	46	$25,000.00	$0.00	$0.00	$11,508.00	$11,508.00	$17,255.00	$17,255.00
2	47	$25,000.00	$0.00	$0.00	$12,635.00	$24,142.00	$18,923.00	$36,178.00
3	48	$25,000.00	$20,344.00	$20,344.00	$23,566.00	$47,709.00	$25,032.00	$61,209.00
4	49	$25,000.00	$23,510.00	$43,854.00	$25,855.00	$73,564.00	$26,837.00	$88,046.00
5	50	$25,000.00	$30,071.00	$73,924.00	$29,916.00	$103,480.00	$29,583.00	$117,629.00
10	55	$25,000.00	$36,406.00	$235,876.00	$37,494.00	$271,651.00	$37,522.00	$286,926.00
15	60	$25,000.00	$46,277.00	$445,093.00	$48,059.00	$489,047.00	$48,091.00	$504,852.00
20	65	$25,000.00	$55,710.00	$698,945.00	$59,869.00	$761,274.00	$60,648.00	$780,701.00
25	70	$0.00	$44,417.00	$901,382.00	$48,360.00	$981,404.00	$49,586.00	$1,006,285.00
30	75	$0.00	$55,958.00	$1,157,393.00	$60,926.00	$1,260,142.00	$62,471.00	$1,292,090.00

*Annual Cash Value Increase and Total Cash Value assume that dividends are paid every year and based on dividend interest rates as of December 2021. Dividends are not guaranteed and can change. The three policy examples on the charts compare three whole-life policies on a healthy forty-five-year-old individual. Results may vary.

This is an actual life insurance illustration based on 2022 dividend scales from a mutually-owned insurance carrier used by the authors.

Policy A:

Your premium goes directly to the death benefit. This design allows for the maximum amount to your beneficiary upon your death but minimizes the policy benefits you can leverage while you are still living.

Policy B:

In Policy B, a Paid-Up Additions Rider is added, allowing your premium to be split between the death benefit and the cash value. This design provides a smaller death benefit short term but increases the benefits that you can Leverage while you are still living, such as accessing the cash value.

Policy A and Policy B can certainly provide you with long-term benefits. However, the whole life policy we recommend is designed to give you maximum cash value in Policy C.

Policy C (The 100 Year Design):

In addition to adding a Paid-Up Additions Rider, Policy C also adds a Term Insurance Rider. Along with the whole life death benefit, the Term Insurance Rider allows you to get as much death benefit as Policy B, at a lower cost. This frees up more dollars to go to the Paid-Up Additions Rider, maximizing the cash value growth.

This special design of a 100 Year policy offers the highest Probability of generating the most cash value, while being a safe-money savings vehicle on the left side of your Barbell.

For this example as well, look closer at Policy C and compare it to the other two scenarios. When starting with a $25,000–contribution in the first year, you'll notice that for your first three years, the overall value increase is relatively modest. However, beginning in the fourth year, all changes—the growth only accelerates from there. By the tenth year, the policy is already quite valuable. By the twentieth year, the exponential growth is clear. This is the value of a whole life policy designed to maximize cash value: easy access to cash throughout the life of the policy and exponential and clear growth without market risk.

COMMON OBJECTIONS TO WHOLE LIFE INSURANCE

Bob had been a typical investor for years, but recently, he became interested in exploring options for whole life insurance products. However, when he took the idea to his financial advisors, he was met with a resounding, "No."

Traditionally, he had trusted these particular advisors, but something about their response bothered him. So, Bob went to get a second opinion from another advisor.

After hearing what Bob wanted and how his advisors had responded, Rubie replied, "You've got advisors telling you this idea is all wrong, but your gut is telling you it's right. Why are you second-guessing yourself? Who is the boss? Whose money is this?"

That was the push Bob needed to hear. He went back to his advisors, put his foot down, and said he would only purchase permanent life insurance products that included the items discussed in this book.

For many investors, this conflict is all too real. They know that a safer path exists—and they may even know what that path looks like—but they keep getting pulled back into the fray by traditionally-minded financial advisors and friends pushing their own agenda. The fact of the matter is that most brokers and advisors aren't keen on selling whole life insurance products. In fact, they'll do just about anything to talk you out of it and sell you another product instead, because they simply don't get paid that much for the "hassle" of selling you a boring old whole life policy.

Your money is your money—not your advisors' money. Building your Barbell means charting your own path and taking total control of your financial destiny by embracing The 100 Year Savings Solution. And to do that, you need the clarity of mind and independence of purpose to demand what you want. In this section, we'll debunk some of the common objections to whole life insurance.

PEOPLE DON'T STICK WITH THEIR POLICIES

Financial analyst Dave Ramsey is on the record saying that he doesn't like insurance products. He has been saying this for many years. In reality, it's not the products themselves that Dave doesn't like; it's that the people who buy them cash their policies out before they mature—and therefore lose money in the process. Dave Ramsey is right. When people do this, they will indeed lose money. In Dave's eyes, why buy a product that you'll have to pay a penalty to get out of down the road?

If this argument sounds familiar, you're right too! This is the exact same argument we make about the dangers of going middle-heavy with IRAs and 401(k)s. Whether you cash out early on a life insurance policy or a retirement plan, the problem isn't with the product itself, but with the buyer's mindset and behavior.

This is why we spent the first half of the book teaching you the tenets of The 100 Year Savings Solution mindset. If you aren't approaching your savings from a long-term perspective, it doesn't matter what savings products you buy; by cashing out early, you surrender all the potential benefits you could have had.

However, if we're playing devil's advocate here, if you *are* going to cash out early, then whole life insurance is still the better bet. When you cash out of a life insurance policy early, you aren't assessed a penalty. With an IRA or a 401(k), you are—to the tune of a 10 percent reduction.

In our experience, the people who purchase a whole life policy rarely have second thoughts or cash out their policies; especially when they have developed the proper mindset as a long-termer. Once they see the power of this product as a savings vehicle, they're more interested in purchasing another policy than they are in replacing it. This is why Rick has eleven policies as of the publishing of this book.

When they *do* end up with second thoughts about their policy, it's usually because their broker recommended against it, not because they were having a bad experience themselves.

The fact is, there's no reason to replace a savings vehicle that carries very little risk, guarantees growth, and is yours to keep once you've passed a minimum threshold of years. Depending on your age, you only need to fund it for seven to ten years, and then the growth it produces could support itself for the rest of your life.

OTHER PRODUCTS HAVE HIGHER RETURNS

Traditional planners will also steer you away from whole life insurance by enticing you with higher potential returns. For instance, they will suggest that you skip the higher premiums of whole life insurance, buy a term life policy instead, and then invest the difference into mutual funds, which they say will bring a 12 percent average annual return.

This sounds good, but here's the thing: while average annual returns are often used as a selling point, in reality, they're nothing more than a smokescreen.

To explain what we mean, let's look at the famous mutual fund, the Fidelity Magellan Fund, that Peter Lynch ran between 1977 and 1990. During that period, Lynch's average annual return on the fund was 29 percent, cementing Lynch as one of the best-performing mutual fund managers in history.

Seeing his success and wanting to generate the same returns for themselves, investors flocked to Lynch's mutual fund. But despite Lynch's long-term success, most of them actually lost money![7]

---

7   Jonathan Dash, "How Investors are Costing Themselves Money," Forbes, June 2, 2021, https://www.forbes.com/sites/forbesfinancecouncil/2021/06/02/how-investors-are-costing-themselves-money/?sh=7c0cd0105e30

So, how could this happen? We already covered the reasons in Chapter 1: we humans are emotional investors, and we tend to buy high and sell low. In the world of mutual funds, this can be disastrous. Say you start with $100,000 in a mutual fund. Over the next few years, it sees big fluctuations in its average annual returns:

- **Year one:** up 25 percent (+$125,000)
- **Year two:** up 100 percent (+$250,000)
- **Year three:** down 75 percent (–$62,500)

Despite two years of strong gains, after just one year of loss, you're in a far worse position than when you started—even though, technically, you had an average annual positive return of 16 percent a year!

When viewed in that light, it's plain to see that looking at average returns doesn't make much sense. You could have a decent average annual return on an investment and still incur a loss. Brokers know this, and they know these numbers can be misleading, but it's still perfectly legal to represent average returns in this way. It's completely factual, but it's just not how money works, and it's not pretty.

When an investment incurs a loss, you don't just lose money as an investor. You also lose opportunity. You lose the potential of what your money could have earned you in the future. Investing in mutual funds can be an effective use of your money but not as an effective left-side strategy.

Besides, the idea that returns on whole life insurance are too low is a common misperception. The reality is that the interest rate on a whole life insurance policy is about the same as an average stock market return, minus taxes—and without the risk.

For the Period Ending 12/31/20

	Average Equity Fund Investor %	Average Fixed Income Investor %	Average Asset Allocation Fund Investor %	S&P 500 %	Bloomberg-Barclays Aggregate Bond Index %	Inflation %
30-Year	7.13	0.34	2.95	10.65	5.29	3.38
20-Year	8.13	0.44	3.57	9.52	4.33	2.32
10-Year	13.44	0.42	6.36	16.55	2.90	2.16
5-Year	14.80	0.80	7.46	18.47	3.57	2.93
3-Year	21.56	1.71	11.60	26.07	4.79	3.53
12-Month	18.39	-1.55	13.29	28.71	-1.54	7.04

Important Disclosures:

Data Sources: Investment Company Institute, Standard & Poor's, Bloomberg Barclays Capital Index Products, and the Bureau of Labor Statistics.

Average investor performance results are calculated using data supplied by the Investment Company Institute. Investor returns are represented by the change in total fund assets after excluding sales, redemptions, and exchanges. This method of calculation captures realized and unrealized capital gains, dividends, interest, trading costs, sales charges, fees, expenses, and any other costs. After calculating investor returns in dollar terms, two percentages are calculated for the period examined: total investor return rate and annualized investor return rate. Total return rate is determined by calculating the investor return dollars as a percentage of the net of the sales, redemptions, and exchanges for each period.

The equity market is represented by the Standard & Poor's 500, an unmanaged index of common stock. The fixed income market is represented by the Bloomberg Barclays Aggregate Bond Index. Inflation is represented by the Consumer Price Index-U. Indexes do not take into account the fees and expenses associated with investing, and individuals cannot invest directly in any index fund. Past performance cannot guarantee future results.

IF YOU INVEST WISELY, YOU DON'T NEED WHOLE LIFE INSURANCE

Whole life insurance *is* investing wisely. First, it builds up your liquid, safe-money assets so you can build the rest of your Barbell with confidence. It provides security, protection, and peace of mind for your family should the unthinkable happen. Second, it's designed to build cash value at a rate of around 4–6 percent interest annually, making it far more valuable than a typical savings account.

Further, the idea that investing wisely means the contemporary approach of going middle- and right-side-heavy is itself a falsehood. As we saw in Chapter 4, there is nothing wise or safe about investing in high-risk assets without a safety net. Such an approach would be antithetical to The 100 Year Mindset.

Remember, the Barbell Strategy isn't an either/or proposition. It's about building your foundation first and *then* exploring other higher-risk investment opportunities that could help you grow your wealth faster. Investing in a whole life policy first gives you the security to pursue other opportunities with confidence. When you approach wealth-building with confidence, you tend to make better decisions. There is a psychological benefit to financial security in the comfort of knowing that you have safe money tucked away that's there for you if you need it.

MY FRIEND TRIED LIFE INSURANCE AND HATED IT

If someone you know felt burned by a life insurance policy, chances are that they purchased a policy that did not suit their needs and wasn't designed in a way that maximized the long-term benefits described herein.

Still, if someone wants to tell you about their bad experience, take the opportunity to learn more. What did they do? How was it set up? Did they buy a whole life policy or a universal life policy?

Many life insurance policies have a guaranteed death benefit but little cash value building up. Many of these policies are linked to the stock market's returns—and therefore linked to risk. In those situations, if the market doesn't perform, the investor is left with nothing after the term is up.

As we discussed earlier, not all whole life policies are the same either. For The 100 Year Savings Solution, we recommend a specific type of policy that comes from a specific type of company.

BROKERS KNOW BEST

Brokers like to say that their number-one job is to recommend the right product for you. With all due respect to brokers and other financial professionals, this is not always the case. Often, they will recommend the product that pays them the most commission.

Whoever you're buying from, it's important that they're honest with you about what products are available, what standard practices are, and what products have the highest benefits to the broker. Absent this discussion, assume that a broker will try to sell you the product that makes them the highest commission, not the one that's the best fit for you.

Often, the approach your broker or advisor will recommend is based on what is known as the 60/40 split in order to diversify your assets. When you're young, the common advice is to put 60 percent of your portfolio in stocks (also known as equities) and 40 percent in bonds. When you're middle-aged, you're advised to create an even split. When you've reached retirement age, you're advised to reverse the split: 40 percent in stocks and 60 percent in bonds.

The thinking behind this approach is that it's a safe way to pursue growth when you're younger and reduce risk when you're older. But let's not mix words: this is bad advice, and we're not the only ones who think so.

First, bonds aren't as safe an investment as they're made out to be. Bond yields are taxable, and they fluctuate in value just like stocks do. In 1993, for instance, long-term bond values dropped 40 percent in a span of only six months. Furthermore, with interest rates at historic lows, bonds won't produce the same investment returns as other safe-money investments.

Second, the Barbell Strategy creates better balance with more diversity and less risk than the traditional 60/40 model ever could. It's lower risk and higher return.

THE MANY BENEFITS OF WHOLE LIFE INSURANCE

Despite the common objections to whole life insurance, it has many benefits that are difficult to find anywhere else. In this section, we'll examine a few of the most unique and most valuable of these benefits.

SETTLE YOUR DEBTS

Logan has built out the right side of his Barbell by loaning money to businesses and businesspeople. A year or so ago, he had loaned a very wealthy (and very elderly) gentleman, Ross, a large amount of money for one of his business ventures. When Ross's business failed to grow as quickly as he had hoped, he found himself unable to pay Logan back. However, he did have a $5 million–whole life insurance policy that had been in place for many years.

Ross called up Logan to propose a new deal. First, he explained his situation. Due to his ill health and his business struggles, he was unable to pay Logan back the money that he owed. Then, he brought up the subject of his life insurance policy. "If you can help me pay the premium, I will add you as a beneficiary, and you will get back everything I owe you. It will come directly from the insurance company at the point of my death."

Logan agreed to Ross's terms and lent him another $30,000 to pay the annual premium on the insurance policy. Sure enough, when Ross's health took a turn for the worse and he died suddenly, Logan received everything he was owed from the insurance company in a timely fashion.

The experience was a huge revelation for Logan. He'd previously thought of life insurance as a pain, and yet here it had just saved him a world of awkward conversations. He was sorry to see Ross pass away, especially since Ross had been a long-term friend, as well as a business partner. However, because Ross had added him as a beneficiary of the insurance policy, which enabled him to receive part of the death benefit, Logan didn't have to worry about straining that relationship by asking Ross's widow for the money he was owed.

BORROWING AGAINST YOUR POLICY

Who would you rather owe money to? The bank or yourself?

In a specially designed whole life insurance policy, your assets are liquid. This means you're free to take money out of your policy whenever you need to in the form of a loan. In effect, you're taking out a loan from yourself. Since you are the owner of the cash in the insurance policy, you become the lender yourself, instead of a bank or a finance company as the lender.

Borrowing against yourself is as simple as calling your insurance company or doing it online with a few clicks of the mouse. If you've been putting $5,000 a month into your policy for a couple of years, you'll have over $100,000 saved up before you know it. If at that point, you need to borrow against your policy for a $20,000-loan to buy a car, all you have to do is call your insurer up, tell them how much you need, and tell them where to send the money.

Again, the basic process isn't unlike financing a car for $45,000 from a dealership. The difference is that you're financing with yourself—which means you can set as favorable terms for yourself as you'd like. Whether you want to pay that money back into your insurance policy over the course of three, four, five years, or more, it's entirely up to you. You're the banker in this scenario; if you need to skip a payment one month, no problem. No penalties, no credit issues, nothing. It's all yours, and it's all penalty-free.

UNINTERRUPTED COMPOUNDING

With whole life insurance, you also get to enjoy the benefits of uninterrupted compounding interest. Rather than rely on the rollercoaster of average annual returns, which are unpredictable from year to year, you know exactly how much your money will grow each year—say 4 percent per year—and that growth will continue uninterrupted until you cash out your policy. This scenario gives you peace of mind.

Even if you borrow against your policy, that growth will continue as if the money was still there. For instance, if you took $45,000 out of your policy to buy a car like in the previous example, that policy still has its full $100,000-cash value. The interest continues to grow on the full $100,000 on the assumption that the $45,000 you borrowed against yourself will be paid back.

If you've ever taken a margin loan on stocks, this is the exact same principle. However, borrowing against a whole life insurance policy is better suited for more long-term loans. For one, most investors don't continually invest in the same stock month after month the way they would in a whole life policy. For another, it's generally not a great idea to amortize a loan over five years on your brokerage account margin debt. There's too much risk involved. If you fall below a certain margin percentage, you'll be asked to pay up—which may be painful to do. At the end of the day, borrowing against your whole life insurance policy is much safer.

SAVINGS THAT WORK FOR YOU

In times of crisis, market crashes, and uncertainty, people often panic. They stop trusting the markets, and they stop trusting the banks, so they liquidate their assets to give themselves cash on hand.

This is a perfectly valid impulse. Just look at some of the biggest companies in the world, like Google, Facebook, or Apple. Combined, those companies are sitting on over $1 trillion in cash. Why? Because they understand the importance of liquidity. As an added benefit, if the market slips and their stocks begin to tumble, they can buy back shares at lower prices and stop the bleeding.

In other words, cash on hand is a good thing, but that doesn't mean you have to park your cash in a low-interest savings account. A whole life insurance policy offers the same security as a savings account, but with 4 percent growth and without any taxes on the gains.

For instance, imagine that you have $1 million sitting in your savings account. If you put that million into a whole life policy, on day one you'll have $2.4 million in life insurance coverage to pay your estate in the event of death. (Please note that this amount may vary from person to person.) Even if you get sick the next day and you desperately want to get your hands on your money, you can still instantly access and receive approximately $850,000 of that insurance money in the form of a loan against your policy. Or, if you want to invest down the road, you can put your money into a whole life policy first, and then borrow from that account to make your investment when the time is right.

YOU CAN BUY IN AT ANY AGE

People are accustomed to thinking that after a certain age, life insurance no longer makes sense for them. This would be true for a term life insurance policy, which doesn't make much sense for most people after the age of seventy, but a whole life policy operates very differently. If you're relatively healthy and younger than eighty-five years of age, then buying a whole life insurance policy can be a fantastic decision.

Term life insurance can be valuable (and we recommend that you have that in certain specific cases). However, whole life insurance valuations are based on the amount of cash in your policy. The insurer takes your money and invests it, while your available cash and death benefit continue to grow. In some cases, it can also be set up as a single-premium policy—meaning you only pay the premium one time. This is perfect if you have a lump sum that you'd like to invest all at once.

Here's what that means. By the time you enter your retirement years, you may have built up a considerable amount of cash savings. But as we just mentioned in the previous section, that money isn't working for you in a traditional savings account. It earns very little interest that way—and what interest it does earn is taxable.

By investing that cash instead into a whole life policy, like The 100 Year Savings Solution, you'll still have instant access to your assets, but will more than likely earn a better return than you would in a traditional savings account. Because whole life policies are guaranteed to grow every year, they may possibly earn an even better return than you would get in the stock market. Further, you can access the money if you have a major health issue, and your money can continue to grow through the magic of uninterrupted compounding.

GIFTING OPPORTUNITIES

Imagine your grandkids twenty, thirty, or even forty years from now. Today, they have the financial freedom to pay for cars, to pay for their education, to make down payments on a house, and to cover other life expenses for the rest of their lives. Why? Because when they were young, you gave them the gift of a whole life insurance policy.

In terms of legacy and lifetime value, there is perhaps no greater gift in the world. As the gift giver, you can safely grow the policy until you choose to transfer control of it to your grandchild. This could be after they've reached a certain age or after you've passed on. The choice is entirely up to you.

WHY HAVE I NEVER HEARD OF THIS?

When seeing such massive potential for growth, you may be wondering why you've never heard about whole life insurance policies like this before. Why isn't your broker pushing it? Why aren't more people buying it? If this is so good, what's the catch?

Here's the short answer: your brokers aren't selling you these policies because they don't make a lot of money off of them.

But you must know that these policies contain hundreds of billions of dollars, and they've been around for more than 100 years. The truth is that they are much more popular and omnipresent than you think.

A whole life policy is designed to give you more cash, which means the insurance company has to look elsewhere in order to make any money off of it—which they usually take from the agents or the broker. Because of the lower commissions, many agents are uninterested in selling these kinds of policies. The ones that *do* sell these kinds of policies usually have a different kind of business model that allows them to better position their clients for wealth accumulation and retirement income—in other words, to help them maximize their savings and have a solid foundation for the long haul.

Furthermore, while a whole life insurance agent may not make

THE 100 YEAR SAVINGS SOLUTION

as much commission on a single policy, they usually sell more policies—often to the same person. The typical insurance broker only sells one policy per person, so they're incentivized to maximize their own profit in the process.

SELECTING THE RIGHT POLICY

The Barbell Investment Strategy is effective because it creates Simplicity, Probability, and Leverage in your savings and wealth-building strategy for a long, long time. However, knowing what you want is one thing; executing it is another. To choose the whole life policy design that is right for you, we recommend speaking with a qualified, 100 Year Team Member to set up your plan. Here are the questions you should ask in order to ensure you get a policy that works for you:

- Is it guaranteed to be there for the rest of my life, or is there a possibility it could fail?
- Does the company guarantee a minimum performance on the policy if I pay my annual premium payments?
- How much experience does the advisor have, both in designing and implementing the policy, and in helping me manage my policy?
- How many of these policies have they sold?
- How many of these policies do they own themselves?
- How many clients have they helped reposition their debt, finance equipment purchases, acquire new businesses, or buy real estate with these policies?

If you're having trouble finding an advisor who offers the kind of whole life insurance products you want, visit our website and schedule a call. We're happy to provide additional resources

124   www.100YearSavings.com

and recommendations to help you get started with your 100 Year Savings Solution. Please visit us on the web at the internet address at the bottom of the page.

GUT CHECK TIME

Congratulations! You now know everything you need to know to make The 100 Year Savings Solution the cornerstone of your financial future. As you start out on this exciting new path, ask yourself:

1. On a scale of 1 to 10, with 10 being the most confident and 1 being the least confident, how would I rate my confidence that I am on the right path to creating long-term wealth for myself and my family?

2. What is stopping me from embracing the values of Simplicity, Probability, and Leverage and getting started on my own 100 Year Saving Solution?

3. What do I believe is my next step?

4. How can this book encourage me to take that next step?

Now that you know the path, remember that you don't have to go it alone. By working with an experienced, like-minded financial partner, you will be able to adapt and apply The 100 Year Savings Solution into your life more quickly and effectively. Schedule a call to get started!

Ready to learn more or talk to our Team? Scan the code above!

Conclusion

Derek ran a successful accounting firm with three locations and seventy employees. After seventeen years in the business, he had successfully learned how to build a business that worked for him and generated income without him having to be a technician.

However, he was at a crossroads with his money. His finances had grown overcomplicated. First, his 401(k) had become too difficult to manage, both for himself and for his company. While it had generated returns in the 7 percent range, it had only done so by taking on tremendous risk. So, while he and his wife had saved up $2 million through his 401(k), he was worried about its safety—and even more concerned that he couldn't access so much of his wealth.

Moving forward, however, was proving tricky. His father, a former Wall Street portfolio manager, had warned him about the dangers of over-allocating into the stock market. But whenever he asked his advisors how he could effectively grow a stable money foundation, they would offer him products that he knew weren't a good fit.

In short, Derek knew there was a better way to save his money. He just didn't know how to get there.

Derek was never introduced to The 100 Year Savings Solution. However, you have been. If you read this book carefully, you will now have knowledge that very few people possess; and you now have the ability to act on that newfound knowledge.

The 100 Year Savings Solution is designed to help create Simplicity, Probability, and Leverage in your life. The Barbell Strategy simplifies your approach, so you always know what your next move is going to be. Because it balances your assets, you have a high Probability of hitting all your objectives. Finally, it allows you to Leverage your existing infrastructure and relationships, so you don't have to step out of your wheelhouse.

We all have weaknesses. For many people, their weakness is their finances. As we said at the very beginning of the book, our very nature often stands in the way of making smart decisions with our money. However, there's a difference between weakness and powerlessness. Systems like the Barbell Strategy are designed to offer protection from our worst impulses so that we can grow our wealth with a sense of confidence and security.

The question is: what path will you take?

Now that you've read this book, you have two options: You can continue on the path you're on, continue to make the same unconscious decisions with your money, and keep getting what you've been getting. Or you can decide on The 100 Year Savings Solution and simplify your financial life.

There is an old proverb that says:

> The master in the art of living makes little distinction between work and play, labor and leisure, mind and body, information and recreation, love, and religion. They hardly know which is which. They simply pursue their vision of excellence at whatever they do, leaving others to decide whether they are at work or at play, since they are always doing both.

Our lives—and especially our financial lives—have become unnecessarily complex. We're always hard at work on the next scheme when we should be focusing on what matters to us and putting all our energy into that. With The 100 Year Savings Solution, you have that opportunity. The rest is up to you.

IT STARTS NOW

Thanks for reading this book!

If the strategy presented in this book appeals to you, schedule your call today. We'll help put you on the path to simplifying your life.

For more information or to get started, visit www.100Year.com.

Acknowledgments

RICK SAPIO

I feel immensely blessed to have been touched by a very long list of solid citizens, many of whom I have already thanked. There is one very special angel that I only recently came to appreciate, more than a decade after her death, and that is Marie Sapio, my Momma. We had a very difficult relationship my entire life. She lost her husband, my dad, to cancer at a very young age. She also lost her son, Frankie, my brother, to cancer, when he was only four years old. I never fully understood the trauma she endured; and as I have journeyed through my own life, I have only recently begun to see her more clearly. Thank you for making a man out of me, Mom!

There are so many others to thank. My wife and I invited 750 people to our wedding, and there are still hundreds more that have touched us in immense ways that we couldn't invite to come; so needless to say, acknowledging all of you is a difficult job. Please know, if you are reading this, then you had, and you continue to have, a positive effect on me.

I do want to thank each of the team members at Scribe. Your professionalism and responsiveness have been off the charts throughout the process of writing this book. Thank you, Tucker, Kacy, Bailey, John, Chas, and Barbara.

My acknowledgments would not be complete without thanking Teresa Kuhn for being such a consistent source of inspiration. Our values have been aligned for such a long time, and I am grateful to call you a colleague, co-author, business partner, and friend.

Recognizing the 100 Year Team, I want to thank Morgan Hunter and Kristin Rusher for helping to build the brand from the ground up. Thanks to the two of you, we've been able to share the 100 Year message with the world.

I also want to thank Mrs. Briggs, my third-grade teacher. You were the first person who told me that I could achieve anything, and you forever changed me, because I believed you whole-heartedly at the age of nine years old.

Most importantly, I want to thank my beautiful and committed wife, Melissa, for always believing in me and our four incredible children.

TERESA KUHN

These acknowledgments reflect my deepest gratitude, and must, then, start with my sincere thanks for all that God has given me. The opportunities have been humbling, and the challenges have been enlightening. With this life I've lived, I know, through God, all things are possible.

I also want to thank my parents. Two Cuban immigrants who sacrificed everything to move to this country. They believed in, and instilled in me, the values of freedom and liberty. They taught me the importance of God, family, and country. I am forever grateful to them, and to my brother, sister, nephew Henry, and his wife, Raechel.

Of course, I am equally grateful to David Kuhn, my former husband. From this union, we had many opportunities to love, serve, and learn from each other. I also want to thank my son, who I adore and love with all my heart. Keating, the privilege of being your mother has been tremendous in every way. The opportunity to launch and grow Gold Eagle Services with both of you has been one of the greatest joys of my life.

Living Wealthy Financial was birthed from my mantra downloaded from God when I was in my teens. I want to express my love and appreciation to Lea Ann Durand, Susan Malochowski, Kristin Rusher, and the rest of the Living Wealthy Financial Team for their trust, love, support, and their unwavering commitment to serving our clients at the highest level. Doing life with all of you has been an honor.

Profound gratitude for the guidance, wisdom, and friendship of Nelson Nash, Tim Austin, Marvin Bulas, and Pamela Yellen and my philosophically aligned colleagues and friends. The path we chose was not an easy one but has been tremendously gratifying.

Tammy de Leeuw, your IQ is off the charts. Profound gratitude for being a comic relief in this crazy world, for your friendship, and for helping me communicate my ideas to the world with your brilliant writing.

And I would be remiss not to thank Rick Sapio and Morgan Hunter, our core team at the 100 Year Company. Launching this brand has been a practice in seeking simplicity in a complex world. That was the origin of the 100 Year brand: Making this time-tested solution and its benefits as simple as possible for thousands of people.

I often talk about a person's need to align their business goals with their values. What I sometimes fail to mention, however, is that it doesn't hurt to have mentors—people who help you discover and clarify your values and gain insights into your life's purpose. They expand your horizons so you can see opportunities you may have missed. Rick Sapio is one of those people for me. It amazes me that two human beings who are polar opposites personality-wise, with different backgrounds and life experiences, can share so much in common. I am grateful for our friendship and business partnership, for always telling me the truth the way you see it and expecting more of me than I do of myself, which is already a very high bar.

There are so many others who have influenced and informed my life; I wish I could acknowledge them all. The coaches, teachers, influencers, friends, amazing conversations, and deep dives have helped me fill in the tiles in this mosaic called my life.

Made in the USA
Middletown, DE
28 March 2023

27818393R00083